Contents

Jerked Tempeh with Herb Rice ....
Lentil and Pumpkin Curry ....
Better-than-Takeout Orange Tofu 8
Tempeh-Stuffed Peppers 8
Vegan Loaded Sweet Potatoes 10
Chimichurri Baked Tofu Bowls 11
Mushroom Taco Bake 12
Blended Golden Milk Latte 13
Granny Smith Green Smoothie 14
Energizing Matcha Smoothie 14
Curried Kale Chips 15
Quick Pickled Carrots and Vegetables 16
Spinach and Mushroom Baked Egg Cups 16
Whole-Grain Carrot Cake Muffins 17
Lemon-Blueberry Yogurt Bowls 19
Triple-Berry Flax Oatmeal 19
Sweet Potato Pancakes 20
Freezer-Friendly Breakfast Burritos 21
Ultimate Vegan Breakfast Sandwiches 23
Broccoli Cheddar Strata 24
Cooling Cucumber-Basil Soup 25
Watermelon Gazpacho 26
10-Minute Miso Soup 26
Vegan Tomato Bisque 27
Creamy Carrot-Ginger Soup 28
Pinto Bean and Tortilla Soup 29
No-Chicken Tofu Noodle Soup 30
Mushroom French Onion Soup 31
Vegan Corn Chowder 33
High-Protein Lentil Soup 33
Broccoli Cheese Soup with Croutons 34
Irish-Inspired Potato Stew 36

- Vegan Gumbo 37
- Pumpkin and Black Bean Chili 37
- Peanut Stew 38
- Green Goddess Cucumber-Avocado Sandwiches 39
- Cranberry and Chickpea Salad Sandwiches 40
- Spicy Peanut-Tofu Lettuce Wraps 41
- Curried Egg Salad Sandwiches 42
- Smoky Lentil and Portobello Mushroom Wraps 43
- Lemon Basil and Smashed White Bean Sandwiches 44
- Loaded Carrot Dogs 44
- Mediterranean Falafel Pitas 46
- Roasted Sweet Potato and Hummus Sandwiches 47
- Vegan Banh Mi Sandwiches 48
- Chickpea and Coconut Curry Wraps 49
- Crispy Eggplant BLTs 50
- Vegan Sushi Burritos 51
- Veggie and White Bean Pesto Melt 51
- Chili-Lime Tempeh Burritos 52
- Freezer-Friendly Bean Burgers 53
- Lentil Sloppy Joes 54
- Mushroom Cheesesteaks 55
- Tempeh Reubens 56
- Buffalo Tofu Sandwiches 57
- Cucumber-Mango Salad 58
- Thai-Inspired Peanut Salad 59
- Strawberry and Avocado Spinach Salad 60
- Red Cabbage and Cilantro Slaw 60
- Make-Ahead Kale Salad 61
- Vegan Greek Salad with Tofu Feta 62
- Caprese Pasta Salad 63
- Creamy Greek Yogurt Potato Salad 64
- Edamame Mason Jar Salad 64
- Vegan Caesar Salad 65

Sun-Dried Tomato and Farro Salad 66

Cranberry, Walnut, and Brussels Sprouts Salad 67

Harvest Butternut Squash and Quinoa Salad 68

Sesame-Ginger Soba Noodle Salad 69

Chili-Lime Taco Salad 70

Zucchini Pasta Primavera 71

15-Minute Cacio e Pepe 72

One-Pot Pantry Pasta 73

Vegan Pad Thai 74

Garlic and Miso Ramen Noodles 75

Tomato-Basil Orecchiette 76

Ginger-Turmeric Rice Noodles 77

Baked Spaghetti Squash Lasagna 78

One-Pot Broccoli Mac and Cheese 79

Five-Spice Noodles 80

One-Pot Creamy Vegan Rigatoni 81

Eggplant Bacon Carbonara 82

Spaghetti and Lentil Balls 84

Creamy Pumpkin-Sage Alfredo 85

Greek Lasagna 86

White Bean and Tomato Stuffed Shells 87

One-Pan Skillet Lasagna 88

Spinach Spaghetti Pie 89

Vegan Cannelloni 90

Cheesy Broccoli Pasta Bake 91

Watermelon Poke Bowls 92

Moroccan-Inspired Chickpea Couscous 93

Pinto Bean Tostadas with Red Cabbage and Cilantro Slaw 94

Vegan Garlic-Mushroom Naan Pizzas 96

Easy Edamame Stir-Fry 97

Roasted Chickpea and Carrot Dinner 98

Sesame Tofu and Broccoli 99

Black Bean Burrito Bowl 100

Apple Chips with Cinnamon-Yogurt Dip 101
Fruit and Nut Energy Bites 101
No-Bake Chocolate–Peanut Butter Bars 102
Sesame-Ginger Edamame 103
Cheesy Vegan Popcorn 104
Chili-Lime Tortilla Chips 105
Roasted Potatoes with Lemon-Chive Yogurt Dip 105
Vegetable Spring Rolls 106
Tofu Nuggets 107
Buffalo Cauliflower 108
Garlicky Roasted Chickpeas 109
Black Bean Quesadillas 110
Pan-Roasted Nachos 111
Baked Potato Skins 112
Vegan Party Platter 113
Chocolate-Covered Mangos 114
Strawberry-Banana Ice Cream 115
Chickpea Cookie Dough 115
Yogurt-Dipped Strawberries 116
Chocolate-Avocado Pudding 117
Snickerdoodle Skillet Cookie 117
Chocolate–Peanut Butter Cups 118
Chai Tea Mug Cake 119
Pumpkin Pie Parfait Jars 120
Vegan No-Bake Blueberry Cheesecake 121
Creamy Oat Milk 122
Vanilla Almond Milk 123
Apple Cider Vinaigrette 123
Sesame Ginger Dressing 124
Lemon Tahini Dressing 125
Spicy Peanut Sauce 126
Rosemary and Thyme Red Sauce 126
Chimichurri Sauce 127

Carrot-Top Pesto	128
Spicy Blender Salsa	129
Chunky Guacamole	129
Vegan Queso Dip	130
Classic Hummus	131
White Bean Sandwich Spread	132
Almond Ricotta	133
Tofu Feta	133
Blueberry Chia Jam	134
Creamy Almond Butter	135
Whole-Grain Croutons	135
Vegan Chocolate Sauce	136
Cinnamon Oat Milk Latte	137
Rejuvenating Citrus Smoothie	138
No-Bake Green Tea Energy Bars	138
Spicy Chickpea-Avocado Toast	139
Apple Pie Granola	140
Peanut Butter and Banana Overnight Oats	141
Tropical Chia Pudding Parfait	142

Jerked Tempeh with Herb Rice

MAKES 2 SERVINGS • PREP TIME: 10 MINUTES • COOK TIME: 10 MINUTES

Ingredients

- 1 (8-ounce) package tempeh
- 1 tablespoon coconut oil, melted, plus more for greasing the skillet
- 2 tablespoons jerk seasoning
- 1 cup cooked brown rice (see Tip)
- ½ cup shredded green cabbage
- ½ cup chopped fresh cilantro
- 1 tablespoon olive oil, or more as needed
- 1 tablespoon fresh lime juice, or more as needed
- Kosher salt

Directions:

Step 1.
Brush the tempeh with the 1 tablespoon melted coconut oil and sprinkle all over with the jerk seasoning.

Step 2.
Lightly grease a large skillet and preheat it over medium heat.

Step 3.
Arrange the seasoned tempeh in a single layer in the skillet and cook for 4 minutes on each side, or until golden and warmed through.

Step 4.
Transfer the tempeh to a cutting board, cut it into strips, and place the strips in a large bowl.

Step 5.
Add the brown rice, cabbage, cilantro, 1 tablespoon olive oil, and 1 tablespoon lime juice.

Step 6.
Taste the mixture and season with salt, and add more oil or lime juice if needed.

Storage: Store the leftovers in an airtight container in the refrigerator for up to 5 days.

Mix it up: Fresh cilantro adds an herbaceous punch to the rice salad served with these Jamaican jerk tempeh strips. If you're not a fan of cilantro, try swapping in fresh parsley instead.

PER SERVING: Calories: 484; Total fat: 27g; Carbohydrates: 41g; Fiber: 4g; Protein: 24g; Calcium: 149mg; Vitamin D: 0mcg; Vitamin B_{12} : 0μg; Iron: 4mg; Zinc: 2mg

Lentil and Pumpkin Curry

MAKES 4 SERVINGS • PREP TIME: 10 MINUTES • COOK TIME: 30 MINUTES

Ingredients

- 2 tablespoons grapeseed oil
- ½ cup diced onion
- 2 medium carrots, diced
- ¼ teaspoon kosher salt
- ¼ teaspoon freshly ground black pepper
- 2 tablespoons curry powder
- 1 cup dried lentils, rinsed
- 1 (13-ounce) can unsweetened coconut milk
- 1 (15-ounce) can pumpkin puree
- 1 cup vegetable broth
- 1 scallion, both white and green parts, chopped
- Fresh cilantro (optional)

Directions:

Step 1.

Heat the oil in a large skillet (that has a lid) over medium heat.

Step 2.

Once the oil is shiny, add the onion, carrots, salt, and pepper, and cook for 5 minutes or until the onion is translucent.

Step 3.

Add the curry powder and cook for 1 minute. Add the lentils, coconut milk, pumpkin, and broth. Cover the skillet, and bring the liquid to a boil.

Step 4.

Reduce the heat to low and simmer for for 20 minutes, stirring occasionally, or until the lentils are tender and the curry is thickened. Add ¼ to ½ cup water if the curry is thickened before the lentils are tender.

Step 5.

Garnish with the chopped scallion and the cilantro, if desired. Serve.

Protein swaps: Instead of dried lentils, use cooked white beans, cubed tofu, or canned chickpeas to get your protein. Dried split peas are another budget-friendly protein option. Just adjust the cooking time and add water as needed to simmer the peas until they're tender.

Storage: Store the leftovers in an airtight container in the refrigerator for up to 5 days.

PER SERVING: Calories: 330; Total fat: 27g; Carbohydrates: 22g; Fiber: 6g; Protein: 6g; Calcium: 82mg; Vitamin D: 0mcg; Vitamin B_{12} : 0μg; Iron: 6mg; Zinc: 1mg

Better-than-Takeout Orange Tofu

MAKES 2 SERVINGS • PREP TIME: 5 MINUTES • COOK TIME: 5 MINUTES

Ingredients

- 1 tablespoon grated orange zest
- 3 tablespoons fresh orange juice
- 1 tablespoon rice vinegar
- 1 tablespoon toasted sesame oil
- 1 tablespoon soy sauce
- 2 tablespoons maple syrup or honey
- 1 teaspoon cornstarch
- 1 teaspoon ground ginger
- 1 recipe Tofu Nuggets, or 1 cup store-bought equivalent
- Red pepper flakes (optional)

Directions:

Step 1.
In a medium bowl, whisk together the orange zest, orange juice, vinegar, sesame oil, soy sauce, maple syrup, cornstarch, and ginger until blended.

Step 2.
Pour the sauce into a large skillet over medium heat. Once it is simmering, add the tofu nuggets and cook for 5 minutes, or until warmed through and the sauce is thickened.

Step 3.
Garnish with the red pepper flakes, if desired, and serve.

Make it easier: Breaded tofu nuggets mimic the crispy fried poultry that's often used for this dish. To make it easier, use plain cubed tofu instead. The texture may be less crispy, but you'll still get all the sweet and tart citrusy flavors.

Storage: Store leftovers in an airtight container in the refrigerator for up to 1 week.

PER SERVING: Calories: 450; Total fat: 27g; Carbohydrates: 40g; Fiber: 3g; Protein: 14g; Calcium: 240mg; Vitamin D: 0mcg; Vitamin B_{12}: 0μg; Iron: 3mg; Zinc: 2mg

Tempeh-Stuffed Peppers

MAKES 2 SERVINGS • PREP TIME: 10 MINUTES • COOK TIME: 35 MINUTES

Ingredients

- 2 bell peppers (any color)
- 2 tablespoons grapeseed oil

- ¼ cup diced onion
- 1 teaspoon ground cumin
- 1 teaspoon ground coriander
- ½ teaspoon smoked paprika
- ¼ teaspoon kosher salt
- ¼ teaspoon freshly ground black pepper
- 1 (16-ounce) package tempeh, crumbled
- ⅔ cup cooked brown rice (see Tip)
- ½ cup frozen corn kernels
- 1 cup chopped fresh or frozen spinach
- ½ cup shredded pepper jack cheese (optional)

Directions:

Step 1.

Preheat the oven to 375°F.

Step 2.

Cut the tops off the bell peppers, scoop out the seeds, and transfer the peppers to an 8-inch glass baking dish.

Step 3.

Heat the oil in a large skillet over medium heat.

Step 4.

Once the oil is shiny, add the onion and cook for 3 minutes, or until translucent.

Step 5.

Add the cumin, coriander, smoked paprika, salt, and pepper and cook for 1 minute.

Step 6.

Add the crumbled tempeh, brown rice, corn, and spinach. Cook for 5 minutes, or until warmed through.

Step 7.

Use the mixture to stuff the bell peppers. Top each pepper with the pepper jack cheese (if using) and bake for 25 minutes, or until the cheese is melted. Serve immediately.

Storage: Store leftovers in an airtight container in the refrigerator for up to 1 week.

Substitute: To make these stuffed peppers vegan, just leave out the pepper jack cheese—there's still plenty of flavor from the tempeh filling on its own. For cheesy flavor without any dairy, try stirring a couple tablespoons of nutritional yeast into the tempeh filling before you stuff the peppers.

PER SERVING: Calories: 617; Total fat: 33g; Carbohydrates: 51g; Fiber: 8g; Protein: 38g; Calcium: 322mg; Vitamin D: 0mcg; Vitamin B_{12} : 0µg; Iron: 8mg; Zinc: 3mg

Vegan Loaded Sweet Potatoes

MAKES 2 SERVINGS • PREP TIME: 5 MINUTES • COOK TIME: 45 MINUTES

Ingredients

- 2 medium sweet potatoes, scrubbed
- 2 tablespoons grapeseed oil
- ¼ cup diced onion
- 1 teaspoon ground cumin
- 1 teaspoon ground coriander
- ½ teaspoon smoked paprika
- ¼ teaspoon kosher salt
- ¼ teaspoon freshly ground black pepper
- 1 (15-ounce) can black beans, drained and rinsed
- 2 cups chopped fresh or frozen spinach
- 1 avocado, peeled, pitted, and diced
- Spicy Blender Salsa or store-bought salsa (optional)

Directions:

Step 1.

Preheat the oven to 450°F.

Step 2.

Pierce the sweet potatoes a few times with a fork and place them on a foil-lined baking sheet. Bake for 45 minutes, or until softened and easily pierced with a fork.

Step 3.

While the potatoes are baking, heat the oil in a large skillet over medium heat.

Step 4.

Once the oil is shiny, add the onion and cook for 3 minutes, or until translucent.

Step 5.

Add the cumin, coriander, smoked paprika, salt, and pepper and cook for 1 minute.

Step 6.

Add the black beans and spinach and cook for 5 minutes, or until warmed through.

Step 7.

Cut the sweet potatoes open lengthwise without cutting through the bottom skin.

Step 8.

Open the potatoes and mash the insides with a fork to create bowls in the center of each half.

Step 9.

Divide the bean mixture between the sweet potatoes. Top with the avocado and serve with the salsa, if desired.

Storage: Store leftovers in an airtight container in the refrigerator for up to 1 week.

Make it easier: Cook the sweet potatoes in the microwave to speed up the cooking time. Pierce the sweet potatoes a few times with a fork, arrange them on a microwave-safe plate, and cook for 5 minutes or until fork-tender.

PER SERVING: Calories: 573; Total fat: 26g; Carbohydrates: 71g; Fiber: 25g; Protein: 21g; Calcium: 299mg; Vitamin D: 0mcg; Vitamin B_{12}: 0µg; Iron: 8mg; Zinc: 3mg

Chimichurri Baked Tofu Bowls

MAKES 2 SERVINGS • PREP TIME: 5 MINUTES • COOK TIME: 30 MINUTES

Ingredients

- ½ (14-ounce) block firm tofu, drained and pressed
- 2 medium carrots, quartered
- 2 cups fresh cauliflower florets
- 2 tablespoons grapeseed oil
- 1 tablespoon apple cider vinegar
- ¼ teaspoon kosher salt
- ¼ teaspoon freshly ground black pepper
- 1½ cups cooked brown rice (see Tip)
- ½ cup Chimichurri Sauce or store-bought sauce

Directions:

Step 1.
Preheat the oven to 450°F. Line a rimmed baking sheet with parchment or a silicone baking mat.

Step 2.
Cut the tofu into 8 pieces and place in a large bowl.

Step 3.
Add the carrots, cauliflower, oil, vinegar, salt, and pepper to the bowl and toss to combine.

Step 4.
Spread the mixture in an even layer on the baking sheet and bake for 30 minutes, flipping halfway through, or until the tofu is golden and crispy.

Step 5.
Place the rice in 2 bowls and add the tofu mixture. Spoon the sauce over each and serve.

Mix it up: The great thing about sauces is that they add tons of flavor to an otherwise neutral dish. This means you can swap out the chimichurri and choose any of all sorts of different tastes. Try sesame oil, rice vinegar, and soy sauce for an Asian-inspired tofu bowl.

Storage: Store the leftovers in an airtight container in the refrigerator for up to 1 week.

PER SERVING: Calories: 896; Total fat: 70g; Carbohydrates: 49g; Fiber: 7g; Protein: 12g; Calcium: 199mg; Vitamin D: 0mcg; Vitamin B_{12} : 0μg; Iron: 5mg; Zinc: 2mg

Mushroom Taco Bake

MAKES 6 SERVINGS • PREP TIME: 10 MINUTES • COOK TIME: 40 MINUTES

Ingredients

- 2 tablespoons grapeseed oil, plus more for greasing the baking dish
- ½ cup diced red onion
- 6 garlic cloves, chopped
- 1 tablespoon ground cumin
- 1 tablespoon ground coriander
- ¼ teaspoon kosher salt
- ⅛ teaspoon freshly ground black pepper
- 2 portobello mushroom caps (about 6 ounces), chopped
- 3 cups cooked black beans
- 1 (28-ounce) can crushed tomatoes
- 12 (4-inch) corn tortillas, halved
- 1½ cups shredded pepper jack cheese

Directions:

Step 1.
Preheat the oven to 425°F and grease an 8-by-11-inch baking dish.

Step 2.
Heat the 2 tablespoons oil in a large skillet over medium heat.

Step 3.
Once the oil is shiny, add the onion and cook for 3 minutes or until translucent.

Step 4.
Add the garlic, cumin, coriander, salt, and pepper and cook for 1 minute.

Step 5.
Add the mushroom caps and cook for 3 minutes, or until darkened.

Step 6.
Add the beans and tomatoes and cook for 5 minutes, or until warmed through.

Step 7.
Spread one-fourth of the bean mixture in the bottom of the baking dish.

Step 8.
Arrange 8 of the tortilla halves on top of the sauce and cover with another one-fourth of the

bean mixture.

Step 9.

Sprinkle ½ cup of the cheese on top.

Step 10.

Repeat layering the ingredients 2 more times, until all the ingredients are used.

1**Directions:**

Step 1.

Transfer the dish to the oven and bake for 25 minutes, or until the cheese is melted. Serve.

Storage: The leftovers can be covered and refrigerated for up to 1 week.

Protein swaps: Instead of black beans, substitute pinto beans, red kidney beans, lentils, crumbled tempeh, or walnuts.

PER SERVING: Calories: 77; Total fat: 15g; Carbohydrates: 45g; Fiber: 13g; Protein: 19g; Calcium: 359mg; Vitamin D: 0mcg; Vitamin B_{12} : 0µg; Iron: 4mg; Zinc: 3mg

Blended Golden Milk Latte

MAKES 2 SERVINGS • PREP TIME: 5 MINUTES

Ingredients

- 3 cups plain Creamy Oat Milk (or milk of choice)
- 1 teaspoon ground turmeric
- ½ teaspoon ground cinnamon
- ¼ teaspoon ground ginger
- ⅛ teaspoon freshly ground black pepper
- 1 teaspoon maple syrup (optional)
- ½ teaspoon vanilla extract (optional)
- Ice cubes, for serving (optional)

Directions:

Step 1.

Place the oat milk, turmeric, cinnamon, ginger, black pepper, and maple syrup and vanilla (if using) in a blender.

Step 2.

Blend on high for 30 seconds, or until the ingredients are well mixed and the oat milk is frothy. Serve over ice, if desired.

Mix it up: Heat the oat milk in the microwave or on the stovetop before you add it to the blender if you want to make this latte hot. Pour in the warm milk carefully and be sure the cover is completely secure whenever you blend hot ingredients.

PER SERVING: Calories: 161; Total fat: 4g; Carbohydrates: 20g; Fiber: 1g; Protein: 13g; Calcium: 467mg; Vitamin D: 4mcg; Vitamin B_{12}: 2µg; Iron: 1mg; Zinc: 2mg

Granny Smith Green Smoothie

MAKES 2 SERVINGS • PREP TIME: 5 MINUTES

Ingredients

- 1 cup frozen spinach
- 1 medium Granny Smith apple, cored and diced
- 1 cup frozen mango chunks
- 1 cup plain Greek yogurt, or more as desired
- ½ teaspoon ground ginger
- ½ teaspoon ground cinnamon
- ½ cup plain Creamy Oat Milk (or milk of choice)

Directions:

Step 1.
Place the spinach, apple, mango, yogurt, ginger, cinnamon, and oat milk in a blender container.

Step 2.
Blend on high for 1 minute or until smooth and creamy. Serve immediately.

Substitute: Any type of frozen fruit works, but I like to use a light-colored variety to keep the color green. Try pineapple or banana if you don't have mango. To make it vegan, use a dairy-free yogurt alternative or mashed avocado in place of the Greek yogurt.

PER SERVING: Calories: 229; Total fat: 6g; Carbohydrates: 36g; Fiber: 6g; Protein: 10g; Calcium: 342mg; Vitamin D: 1mcg; Vitamin B_{12}: 1µg; Iron: 2mg; Zinc: 2mg

Energizing Matcha Smoothie

MAKES 2 SERVINGS • PREP TIME: 5 MINUTES

Ingredients

- 2 cups frozen mango chunks
- ½ cup frozen spinach
- 2 tablespoons chia seeds
- 1 tablespoon matcha
- 2 cups plain Creamy Oat Milk (or milk of choice)

- 1 teaspoon vanilla extract (optional)
- 2 teaspoons maple syrup or sweetener of choice (optional)

Directions:

Step 1.

Place the mango, spinach, chia seeds, matcha, oat milk, and vanilla and maple syrup (if using) in a blender.

Step 2.

Blend on high for 1 minute, or until smooth and creamy. Serve.

Substitute: If you don't have oat milk, try this smoothie with whatever type of milk you have on hand. Opt for soy or cow's milk if you want to add more protein. For an additional boost, try this recipe with a tablespoon of ground flaxseed.

PER SERVING: Calories: 282; Total fat: 8g; Carbohydrates: 44g; Fiber: 9g; Protein: 13g; Calcium: 463mg; Vitamin D: 3mcg; Vitamin B_{12} : 1µg; Iron: 2mg; Zinc: 2mg

Curried Kale Chips

MAKES 4 SERVINGS • PREP TIME: 10 MINUTES • COOK TIME: 50 MINUTES

Ingredients

- ¼ cup tahini
- 1 tablespoon curry powder
- 1 teaspoon maple syrup
- ¼ teaspoon kosher salt
- 4 tablespoons water
- 1 pound fresh kale

Directions:

Step 1.

Preheat the oven to 275°F. Line 2 baking sheets with parchment.

Step 2.

In a large bowl, whisk together the tahini, curry powder, maple syrup, and salt until blended. Gradually add the water until the sauce is thinned.

Step 3.

Tear the kale leaves from the stems and toss them in the bowl with the tahini sauce. Use your hands to toss the kale pieces until they're evenly coated. Spread the kale in a single layer on the baking sheets.

Step 4.

Bake the chips for 50 minutes or until dry and crispy. Cool them on a rack.

Storage: Store the chips in an airtight container at room temperature for up to 1 week.

Mix it up: You can use all sorts of spice blends to flavor kale chips. Try sweet and spicy Jamaican jerk seasoning, cheesy nutritional yeast, or Cajun spices. Instead of tahini, use peanut butter or any nut butter you happen to have on hand.

PER SERVING: Calories: 154; Total fat: 9g; Carbohydrates: 15g; Fiber: 6g; Protein: 8g; Calcium: 244mg; Vitamin D: 0mcg; Vitamin B_{12} : 0μg; Iron: 3mg; Zinc: 1mg

Quick Pickled Carrots and Vegetables

MAKES 4 SERVINGS • PREP TIME: 10 MINUTES

Ingredients

- 1 cup thinly sliced carrots
- 2 jalapeño peppers, thinly sliced
- 1 tablespoon kosher salt
- 1 tablespoon sugar
- 1 tablespoon cumin seeds (optional)
- ½ cup water
- ½ cup rice vinegar

Directions:

Step 1.
Place the carrots and jalapeños in a pint glass jar with a lid. Add the salt, sugar, cumin seeds (if using), water, and vinegar. Cover the jar and shake to mix.

Step 2.
Refrigerate the mixture for at least 30 minutes, or until the vegetables have softened and are flavored by the pickling liquid. Taste and add more salt or sugar as needed.

Step 3.
Cover the jar again and refrigerate until ready to use.

Storage: The pickles will keep in the covered jar, refrigerated, for up to 3 months.

Mix it up: If you're not a fan of jalapeños, try making pickled vegetables with radishes, cucumbers, beets, or red onions. You can also change the pickling spices. Try adding herbs, such as chives or dill, or coriander seeds.

PER SERVING: Calories: 29; Total fat: 0g; Carbohydrates: 6g; Fiber: 1g; Protein: 0g; Calcium: 14mg; Vitamin D: 0mcg; Vitamin B_{12} : 0μg; Iron: 0mg; Zinc: 0mg

Spinach and Mushroom Baked Egg Cups

MAKES 6 SERVINGS • PREP TIME: 10 MINUTES • COOK TIME: 20 MINUTES

Ingredients

- Grapeseed oil or nonstick cooking spray
- 1 cup chopped fresh baby spinach
- 1 cup sliced button mushrooms
- 1 cup shredded mozzarella cheese
- 12 large eggs
- 2 teaspoons dried oregano
- ½ teaspoon red pepper flakes (optional)
- ¼ teaspoon kosher salt

Directions:

Step 1.

Preheat the oven to 350°F. Lightly grease 6 cups of a 12-cup muffin tin.

Step 2.

Divide the spinach, mushrooms, and mozzarella among 6 cups of the muffin tin. In a medium bowl, beat the eggs (whisk until no longer streaky), then add the oregano, red pepper flakes (if using), and salt. Divide the egg mixture among the muffin cups, leaving a ¼-inch space at the top of the cups for the eggs to rise. (If desired, pour the beaten eggs into a liquid measuring cup for easier pouring.) Bake the cups for 20 minutes, or until golden brown and puffy.

Step 3.

Allow the egg cups to cool slightly before removing with a spatula and transferring them to a plate. Serve.

Storage: Place the egg cups in an airtight container and refrigerate for up to 4 days or freeze for up to 6 months.

Mix it up: You can use many different fresh, frozen, and canned vegetables to make baked egg cups. Any type of cheese will also work for this recipe. For Mexican-inspired flavors, try substituting tomatoes, peppers, and cheddar jack cheese.

PER SERVING: Calories: 205; Total fat: 14g; Carbohydrates: 2g; Fiber: g; Protein: 17g; Calcium: 161mg; Vitamin D: 4mcg; Vitamin B_{12} : 1μg; Iron: 2mg; Zinc: 2mg

Whole-Grain Carrot Cake Muffins

MAKES 12 MUFFINS • PREP TIME: 15 MINUTES • COOK TIME: 15 MINUTES

Ingredients

- Grapeseed oil or nonstick cooking spray

- 1¾ cups whole wheat flour
- 2 teaspoons ground cinnamon
- 1½ teaspoons baking powder
- ½ teaspoon ground ginger
- ½ teaspoon baking soda
- ½ teaspoon kosher salt
- 2 cups grated carrots
- ½ cup walnut halves and pieces
- 2 large eggs
- 1 cup plain or vanilla Greek yogurt
- ⅓ cup unsweetened applesauce
- ⅓ cup maple syrup

Directions:

Step 1.
Preheat the oven to 425°F and grease a 12-cup muffin tin.

Step 2.
In a large bowl, stir together the flour, cinnamon, baking powder, ginger, baking soda, and salt until well blended. Fold in the carrots and walnuts.

Step 3.
In a medium bowl, beat the eggs until well blended Add the yogurt, applesauce, and maple syrup.

Step 4.
Pour the liquid ingredients into the bowl of dry ingredients and stir until just combined.

Step 5.
Divide the batter among the cups of the muffin tin (about 1/3 cup batter per cup). Bake the muffins for 15 minutes, or until they are golden on top and an inserted toothpick comes out clean.

Step 6.
Remove the muffins from the oven and allow them to cool in the pan for 5 minutes, then transfer to a metal rack to cool completely. If the muffins are sticking to the pan, slide a butter knife around the edges to loosen them. Serve.

Storage: Place the muffins in an airtight container and store at room temperature for up to 2 days, in the refrigerator for up to 4 days, or in the freezer for up to 3 months.

Tip: Make this recipe easier by purchasing shredded carrots at the grocery store. If you have a shredding attachment, you can also use your food processor to shred the whole carrots.

PER SERVING (1 MUFFIN): Calories: 147; Total fat: 5g; Carbohydrates: 23g; Fiber: 3g; Protein: 6g; Calcium: 82mg; Vitamin D: 0mcg; Vitamin B_{12} : 0µg; Iron: 1mg; Zinc: 1mg

Lemon-Blueberry Yogurt Bowls

MAKES 2 SERVINGS • PREP TIME: 5 MINUTES

Ingredients

- 2 cups plain or vanilla Greek yogurt
- 2 tablespoons ground flaxseed (optional)
- 2 teaspoons grated lemon zest (reserve some for topping, if desired)
- 1 tablespoon fresh lemon juice
- ½ teaspoon ground cinnamon (optional)
- ½ teaspoon vanilla extract (optional)
- 1 cup (about 6 ounces) fresh blueberries (or use thawed frozen berries)
- ¼ cup chopped almonds, toasted if desired
- 2 to 4 teaspoons maple syrup or honey (depending on desired sweetness)

Directions:

Step 1.

In a medium bowl, stir together the yogurt, flaxseed (if using), lemon zest, lemon juice, and cinnamon and vanilla (if using).

Step 2.

Divide the mixture between 2 bowls or jars and top with the blueberries and almonds.

Step 3.

Drizzle with maple syrup or honey and garnish with the remaining grated lemon zest, if desired.

Tip: Make this dish easier with store-bought lemon juice; skip the grated lemon zest if you choose this route. You can also buy sliced or chopped almonds to cut out some of the meal prep.

PER SERVING: Calories: 211; Total fat: 8g; Carbohydrates: 27g; Fiber: 0g; Protein: 9g; Calcium: 308mg; Vitamin D: 0mcg; Vitamin B_{12}: 1μg; Iron: 0mg; Zinc: 2mg

Triple-Berry Flax Oatmeal

MAKES 1 SERVING • PREP TIME: 5 MINUTES • COOK TIME: 2 MINUTES

Ingredients

- 1 cup unsweetened soy milk (or milk of choice)
- ½ cup old-fashioned rolled oats
- 2 tablespoons ground flaxseed
- ½ teaspoon ground cinnamon

- ⅛ teaspoon ground ginger (optional)
- ⅛ teaspoon kosher salt
- ½ cup frozen triple berry blend (strawberries, raspberries, blackberries)

Directions:

Step 1.

In a medium microwave-safe bowl, stir together the soy milk, oats, flaxseed, cinnamon, ginger (if using), and salt. Add the frozen triple berry blend.

Step 2.

Cover the bowl, allowing the corner to vent, and microwave on high for 1 minute and 30 seconds. Stir, replace the cover, and microwave on high for an additional 30 seconds, or until the berries are warm and the oats are softened. Stir again and allow the oatmeal to cool and thicken for a couple of minutes before serving.

Mix it up: Change the type of fruit and spices to give this microwavable oatmeal bowl a whole new taste. Try the tropical fruits from the Tropical Chia Pudding Parfait or make this with frozen diced apples or pears.

PER SERVING: Calories: 523; Total fat: 14g; Carbohydrates: 79g; Fiber: 15g; Protein: 24g; Calcium: 414mg; Vitamin D: 3mcg; Vitamin B_{12} : 1μg; Iron: 5mg; Zinc: 5mg

Sweet Potato Pancakes

MAKES 2 SERVINGS • PREP TIME: 5 MINUTES • COOK TIME: 10 MINUTES

Ingredients

- 1 small sweet potato
- ½ cup unsweetened soy milk (or milk of choice)
- 1 large egg
- 1 tablespoon maple syrup
- 1 teaspoon vanilla extract
- ½ cup whole wheat flour
- ½ teaspoon baking powder
- ½ teaspoon ground cinnamon
- ¼ teaspoon ground ginger
- ¼ teaspoon kosher salt
- Grapeseed oil or nonstick cooking spray

OPTIONAL FOR SERVING

- Maple syrup
- Chopped nuts, such as pecans or walnuts
- Greek yogurt or whipped cream

Directions:

Step 1.

Pierce the sweet potato with a fork, wrap it in a paper towel, and microwave on high for 5 minutes, or until softened. Allow the sweet potato to cool enough to handle. Slice it in half and use a spoon to scoop out the flesh into a large bowl, then mash with a potato masher or fork. You should have around ⅓ cup mashed sweet potato.

Step 2.

Add the soy milk, egg, maple syrup, and vanilla to the sweet potato and whisk until combined. It's okay if there are some lumps of sweet potato.

Step 3.

Gradually add the flour while stirring constantly.

Step 4.

Add the baking powder, cinnamon, ginger, and salt.

Step 5.

Heat a large greased or nonstick skillet over medium heat. Pour about ¼ cup of the batter into the skillet, cooking 2 pancakes at a time. Cook for 3 minutes, or until bubbles begin to form. Flip and cook for 2 minutes more, or until golden.

Step 6.

Transfer the cooked pancakes to a plate and keep warm. Clean and grease the skillet again as needed. Repeat with the remaining batter, cooking another batch of 2 pancakes. Turn down the heat if the bottoms turn brown before the center is cooked.

Step 7.

Serve the pancakes with maple syrup, chopped nuts, and yogurt or whipped cream, if desired.

Storage: Store leftover pancakes in an airtight container in the refrigerator for up to 5 days or freeze for up to 2 months.

Make it easier: Substitute canned pumpkin puree for the sweet potato in this recipe. You can skip the first step and add the pumpkin right to the bowl and start mixing with the other ingredients.

PER SERVING (2 PANCAKES): Calories: 255; Total fat: 4g; Carbohydrates: 46g; Fiber: 6g; Protein: 10g; Calcium: 192mg; Vitamin D: 2 mcg; Vitamin B_{12} : 1mcg; Iron: 2mg; Zinc: 2mg

Freezer-Friendly Breakfast Burritos

MAKES 6 SERVINGS • PREP TIME: 25 MINUTES • COOK TIME: 20 MINUTES

Ingredients

- 2 tablespoons grapeseed oil, or more as needed

- 1 small onion, diced
- 1 bell pepper (any color), seeded, cored, and diced
- 3 jalapeño peppers, sliced (optional; remove ribs and seeds for mild flavor)
- 2 cups cooked black beans
- 1 tablespoon chili powder
- 1 tablespoon ground cumin
- Kosher salt
- 10 large eggs, lightly beaten
- 6 large flour tortillas
- 1 cup shredded cheddar cheese (optional)
- ¾ cup chopped scallions, both white and green parts (1 bunch; optional)

Directions:

Step 1.
Heat the oil in a large skillet over medium heat. Once the oil is shiny, add the onion and cook for 4 minutes, or until translucent.

Step 2.
Add the bell pepper, jalapeños (if using), black beans, chili powder, cumin, and salt. Cook for 5 minutes, or until the peppers are softened, stirring occasionally. Transfer the mixture to a bowl or plate.

Step 3.
Reduce the heat to medium-low and add more oil to the skillet if needed. Pour in the beaten eggs and cook for 8 minutes, stirring occasionally, or until no liquid remains and the eggs are cooked all the way through. Remove the skillet from the heat.

Step 4.
To assemble the burritos, warm the tortillas for 20 seconds in the microwave (in batches of 2 to 3), then lay a tortilla on a flat surface.

Step 5.
Spread one-sixth of the bean and vegetable mixture in the center of the tortilla.

Step 6.
Spoon one-sixth of the cooked eggs on top.

Step 7.
Sprinkle some of the cheese and scallions (if using) on top.

Step 8.
Roll the tortilla up and wrap it with parchment paper or aluminum foil.

Step 9.
Repeat with the remaining tortillas until all the ingredients are used. Once you have finished, place the wrapped burritos in a freezer-safe bag and freeze.

Step 10.

To reheat, unwrap one of the burritos, place it on a damp paper towel–lined plate, and microwave on high for 3 minutes.

Tip: Omit the eggs and cheese to make these breakfast burritos vegan. You can also use scrambled tofu instead of the eggs and nutritional yeast instead of the cheese if you want to keep the protein content similar to the original recipe.

PER SERVING: Calories: 345; Total fat: 15g; Carbohydrates: 34g; Fiber: 7g; Protein: 19g; Calcium: 121mg; Vitamin D: 2mcg; Vitamin B_{12} : 1µg; Iron: 4mg; Zinc: 2mg

Ultimate Vegan Breakfast Sandwiches

MAKES 2 SANDWICHES • PREP TIME: 30 MINUTES • COOK TIME: 8 MINUTES

Ingredients

- 2 tablespoons grapeseed oil
- ½ teaspoon garlic powder
- ½ teaspoon onion powder
- ½ teaspoon ground turmeric
- Kosher salt
- Freshly ground black pepper
- 1 (14-ounce) block extra-firm tofu, drained, pressed (see Tip), and cut into rectangles
- 4 slices whole-grain bread (or 2 sliced bagels or English muffins), toasted if desired
- ½ cup fresh baby spinach (or lettuce of choice)
- ½ red bell pepper, sliced into strips
- 1 avocado, peeled, pitted, and sliced

Directions:

Step 1.

In a medium bowl, whisk together the oil, garlic powder, onion powder, and turmeric, and season with salt and pepper.

Step 2.

Place a large skillet over medium heat.

Step 3.

Dip the tofu pieces in the oil mixture to coat them and then spread the tofu in the skillet. Cook for 5 minutes, or until the tofu separates easily from the pan.

Step 4.

Flip and cook for an additional 3 minutes, or until the other side of the tofu separates easily from the pan.

Step 5.

Lay 2 slices of bread (or one half of 2 bagels or English muffins) on a flat surface.

Step 6.

Divide the spinach, red bell pepper slices, avocado, and cooked tofu between the bread slices. Place the remaining pieces of bread (or other half of the bagel or English muffin) on top of each.

Step 7.

Cut the sandwiches in half if desired and serve.

Protein swaps: Substitute scrambled or fried eggs if you include them in your diet. If you're looking for another plant-based alternative, try mashed chickpeas or cannellini beans.

PER SERVING (1 SANDWICH): Calories: 670; Total fat: 45g; Carbohydrates: 44g; Fiber: 14g; Protein: 34g; Calcium: 478mg; Vitamin D: 0mcg; Vitamin B_{12}: 0µg; Iron: 7mg; Zinc: 4mg

Broccoli Cheddar Strata

MAKES 6 SERVINGS • PREP TIME: 10 MINUTES • COOK TIME: 55 MINUTES

Ingredients

- Grapeseed oil or nonstick cooking spray
- 6 large eggs
- 2 cups milk
- ½ teaspoon garlic powder (or 4 garlic cloves)
- ½ teaspoon kosher salt
- ¼ teaspoon freshly ground black pepper
- 2½ cups chopped broccoli florets
- 2½ cups torn leftover bread (from about ½ loaf)
- 1 cup (8 ounces) shredded cheddar cheese

Directions:

Step 1.

Preheat the oven to 350°F and grease an 8-by-11-inch glass baking dish.

Step 2.

In a large bowl, whisk the eggs, milk, garlic powder, salt, and pepper until no longer streaky.

Step 3.

Add the broccoli, bread, and cheese.

Step 4.

Pour the mixture into the baking dish, spreading it out evenly, and bake uncovered for 55 minutes or until the center is set and the top is golden.

Step 5.

Cool the strata for at least 5 minutes before slicing it into 6 pieces.

Mix it up: You can change the vegetables and type of cheese to create endless flavor combinations for the strata. Try butternut squash with goat cheese or spinach and mushrooms with mozzarella.

Storage: Store leftover strata pieces in an airtight container in the refrigerator for up to 4 days.

PER SERVING: Calories: 254; Total fat: 14g; Carbohydrates: 17g; Fiber: 2g; Protein: 17g; Calcium: 297mg; Vitamin D: 2mcg; Vitamin B$_{12}$: 1µg; Iron: 2mg; Zinc: 2mg

Cooling Cucumber-Basil Soup

MAKES 2 SERVINGS • PREP TIME: 5 MINUTES

Ingredients

- 1 large English cucumber, peeled and chopped
- ½ cup plain Greek yogurt
- ⅓ cup fresh basil, plus extra for serving
- 2 tablespoons fresh lemon juice
- 1 garlic clove, chopped
- 2 tablespoons olive oil, plus additional for serving
- Kosher salt
- Freshly ground black pepper

Directions:

Step 1.
Place the cucumber, Greek yogurt, basil, lemon juice, garlic, and olive oil in a blender and pulse 10 times, or until the soup is creamy.

Step 2.
Taste and season with salt and pepper, if needed.

Step 3.
Divide the soup between 2 bowls and drizzle with olive oil and fresh basil leaves, if desired.

Tip: Greek yogurt is a type of strained yogurt that's thicker and higher in protein than other common yogurt varieties. You can substitute Icelandic skyr for a similar result. Regular and nondairy yogurts also work, especially if you're looking for a lighter, more drinkable soup.

Storage: Store leftover soup in an airtight container in the refrigerator for up to 2 days.

PER SERVING: Calories: 180; Total fat: 16g; Carbohydrates: 8g; Fiber: 1g; Protein: 3g; Calcium: 104mg; Vitamin D: 0mcg; Vitamin B$_{12}$: 0µg; Iron: 1mg; Zinc: 1mg

Watermelon Gazpacho

MAKES 4 SERVINGS • PREP TIME: 10 MINUTES

Ingredients

- 4 cups chopped seedless watermelon
- 1¼ cups chopped English cucumber (½ medium)
- 1 red bell pepper, seeded, cored, and chopped
- ¼ cup fresh parsley leaves
- 1 garlic clove, minced
- 1 teaspoon grated lemon zest (from 1 medium)
- 2 tablespoons fresh lemon juice (from 1 medium)
- Kosher salt
- Freshly ground black pepper

Directions:

Step 1.
Put the watermelon, cucumber, bell pepper, parsley, garlic, lemon zest, and lemon juice in a blender and pulse 5 times, or until the soup is liquid-like, but not totally pureed.

Step 2.
Season to taste with salt and pepper. Serve.

Storage: Store leftover soup in an airtight container in the refrigerator for up to 1 week.

Substitute: Try making this gazpacho with fresh tomatoes if watermelon isn't available in your area. You can also try making it with other fresh fruits, such as strawberries.

PER SERVING: Calories: 60; Total fat: 0g; Carbohydrates: 14g; Fiber: 1g; Protein: 2g; Calcium: 25mg; Vitamin D: 0mcg; Vitamin B_{12}: 0µg; Iron: 1mg; Zinc: 0mg

10-Minute Miso Soup

MAKES 1 SERVING • PREP TIME: 5 MINUTES • COOK TIME: 5 MINUTES

Ingredients

- ¼ cup frozen shelled edamame (massage the bag to help separate the beans)
- ¼ cup diced fresh shiitake or cremini mushrooms
- 1 small scallion, both white and green parts, chopped
- 1½ cups water
- 1½ tablespoons miso paste
- Sesame seeds (optional)

Directions:

Step 1.

Stir together the edamame, mushrooms, scallion, and water in a large, microwave-safe mug or bowl. Place a paper towel on top and microwave on high for 2 minutes.

Step 2.

Carefully remove the bowl from the microwave and stir.

Step 3.

Spoon the miso paste into a small bowl.

Step 4.

Pour about ¼ cup liquid from the cooked soup into the miso and use a fork or small whisk to mix.

Step 5.

Pour the miso mixture into the soup and stir until evenly mixed.

Step 6.

Garnish with sesame seeds, if desired, and serve immediately.

Substitute: If you don't have mushrooms, try substituting broccoli or baby bok choy for the vegetables in this soup. Frozen (blanched and chopped) vegetables are also convenient options because you can add them to the soup without thawing.

PER SERVING: Calories: 181; Total fat: 4g; Carbohydrates: 31g; Fiber: 7g; Protein: 10g; Calcium: 53mg; Vitamin D: 1mcg; Vitamin B_{12} : 0μg; Iron: 2mg; Zinc: 3mg

Vegan Tomato Bisque

MAKES 4 SERVINGS • PREP TIME: 5 MINUTES • COOK TIME: 25 MINUTES

Ingredients

- 2 tablespoons grapeseed oil
- 1 small onion, diced (about ¾ cup)
- 3 garlic cloves, smashed
- 2 cups vegetable broth
- 1 (28-ounce) can crushed tomatoes
- 1 tablespoon dried basil
- 1 teaspoon dried thyme
- 2 cups plain unsweetened soy milk (or plain dairy-free milk of choice)
- Kosher salt
- Freshly ground black pepper

Directions:

Step 1.

Heat the oil in a 12-quart stockpot over medium heat. Once the oil is shiny, add the onion and cook for 4 minutes, stirring often, or until onion is translucent.

Step 2.

Add the garlic and cook for an additional minute.

Step 3.

Add the broth, tomatoes, basil, and thyme.

Step 4.

Bring the soup to a boil, reduce the heat to low, and simmer for 10 minutes, or until the onion is softened.

Step 5.

Add the soy milk and season with salt and pepper. Warm briefly, then remove the pot from the heat.

Step 6.

Taste the soup and adjust the seasonings as desired.

Step 7.

Transfer the soup in batches to a blender and pulse until the soup is smooth and creamy. Pulse only a few times if you want the soup to have a chunkier texture.

Step 8.

Transfer the pureed soup to a large bowl as you process the batches. Serve.

Storage: Store leftover soup in an airtight container in the refrigerator for up to 1 week or freeze for up to 3 months.

Substitute: If you include dairy in your lifestyle, substitute cow's milk for the soy milk in this recipe. Other plant milk varieties also work; just make sure they're unsweetened and plain (not vanilla flavored).

PER SERVING: Calories: 214; Total fat: 9g; Carbohydrates: 30g; Fiber: 5g; Protein: 7g; Calcium: 194mg; Vitamin D: 1mcg; Vitamin B_{12} : 1µg; Iron: 5mg; Zinc: 1mg

Creamy Carrot-Ginger Soup

MAKES 4 SERVINGS • PREP TIME: 15 MINUTES • COOK TIME: 30 MINUTES

Ingredients

- 2 tablespoons grapeseed oil, or more as needed
- 1 small onion, diced
- 3 cups diced carrots
- 1 small sweet potato, peeled and diced
- 1 (1½-inch) piece of fresh ginger, peeled and grated

- 3 garlic cloves, chopped
- 1 teaspoon ground turmeric (optional)
- 2 cups vegetable broth
- 1 (13.6-ounce) can unsweetened coconut milk
- Kosher salt
- Freshly ground black pepper

Directions:

Step 1.

Heat the 2 tablespoons oil in a 12-quart stockpot over medium heat. Once the oil is shiny, add the onion and cook for 4 minutes, stirring often, or until the onion is translucent.

Step 2.

Add the carrots, sweet potato, ginger, garlic, and turmeric (if using), then cook for 10 minutes.

Step 3.

Add more oil or adjust the heat if the vegetables are sticking to the pan or starting to burn.

Step 4.

Add the broth and coconut milk. Bring the soup to a boil, reduce the heat to low, and cook for 10 minutes, or until the carrots and sweet potato are tender.

Step 5.

Season with salt and pepper to taste. Remove the soup from the heat.

Step 6.

Transfer the soup in batches to a blender and blend for 30 seconds or until the soup is smooth and creamy. Transfer the pureed soup to a large bowl as you process the batches. Serve.

Storage: Store leftover soup in an airtight container and refrigerate for up to 1 week or freeze for up to 3 months.

Tip: You can make the soup prep easier by swapping in frozen chopped carrots for the fresh ones in this recipe. Canned carrots are another option if you'd like to do less chopping.

PER SERVING: Calories: 337; Total fat: 28g; Carbohydrates: 23g; Fiber: 4g; Protein: 4g; Calcium: 68mg; Vitamin D: 0mcg; Vitamin B_{12} : 0μg; Iron: 4mg; Zinc: 1mg

Pinto Bean and Tortilla Soup

MAKES 6 SERVINGS • PREP TIME: 10 MINUTES • COOK TIME: 25 MINUTES

Ingredients

- 2 tablespoons grapeseed oil, or more as needed

- 1 small white onion, diced
- 2 medium carrots, diced
- 1 or 2 jalapeño peppers, chopped (remove seeds, if desired)
- 3 garlic cloves, chopped
- 1 tablespoon ground cumin
- 1 tablespoon chili powder
- Kosher salt
- 1 (28-ounce) can crushed tomatoes
- 4 cups vegetable broth
- 6 (5-inch) corn tortillas, cut into 1-inch pieces
- 2 (15-ounce) cans pinto beans, drained and rinsed

Directions:

Step 1.

Heat the 2 tablespoons oil in a 12-quart stockpot over medium heat. Once the oil is shiny, add the onion and cook for 4 minutes, stirring often, or until the onion is translucent.

Step 2.

Add the carrots, jalapeños, garlic, cumin, and chili powder. Season to taste with salt and cook for an additional 5 minutes. Add more oil if needed to prevent sticking.

Step 3.

Add the tomatoes and broth and increase the heat to high. Bring the soup to a boil, reduce the heat to low, and add the tortillas. Simmer the soup for 10 minutes.

Step 4.

Transfer the soup in batches to a blender and blend for 30 seconds or until the soup is smooth and creamy. Transfer the soup to a large bowl as you process the batches.

Step 5.

Add the pinto beans. Serve.

Storage: Store leftover soup in an airtight container in the refrigerator for up to 1 week.

Protein swaps: If you want to switch out the pinto beans, canned black beans make an ideal substitute. You can also use cooked tofu, tempeh, or lentils to round out this dish with a good source of plant-based protein.

PER SERVING: Calories: 304; Total fat: 7g; Carbohydrates: 54g; Fiber: 13g; Protein: 12g; Calcium: 136mg; Vitamin D: 0mcg; Vitamin B_{12} : 0μg; Iron: 6mg; Zinc: 2mg

No-Chicken Tofu Noodle Soup

MAKES 4 SERVINGS • PREP TIME: 10 MINUTES • COOK TIME: 20 MINUTES

Ingredients

- 2 tablespoons grapeseed oil
- 1 small onion, diced
- 1 large carrot, diced
- 2 celery stalks, diced
- 4 garlic cloves, chopped
- 1 tablespoon dried thyme
- 1 (14-ounce) block extra-firm tofu, drained, pressed (see Tip), and chopped
- 4 cups vegetable broth
- 2 ounces dried whole wheat spaghetti (or other pasta of choice)
- 1 cup water (optional)
- ⅓ cup chopped fresh parsley (optional)
- Kosher salt
- Freshly ground black pepper

Directions:

Step 1.

Heat the oil in a 12-quart stockpot over medium heat. Once the oil is shiny, add the onion, carrot, and celery, and cook for 5 minutes, or until the onion is translucent.

Step 2.

Add the garlic and thyme and cook for an additional 1 minute.

Step 3.

Add the chopped tofu and vegetable broth. Increase the heat to high, cover, and bring to a boil. Add the spaghetti and cook for 8 minutes, or until al dente.

Step 4.

If there's not enough liquid, pour in the water as needed.

Step 5.

Add the parsley (if using) and season with salt and pepper to taste. Serve.

Storage: Store leftover soup in an airtight container in the refrigerator for up to 1 week. Add more water before reheating if there isn't enough broth.

Tip: To prepare a block of tofu, drain the liquid, wrap it in a towel, and press it by placing something heavy (such as a cast iron skillet) on top for at least 30 minutes.

Protein swaps: Substitute 2 cups cooked chickpeas or cannellini beans for the tofu, if desired. You can also substitute dried lentils for a budget-friendly option. If you use lentils, boil them for about 8 minutes before adding the pasta to the pot.

PER SERVING: Calories: 232; Total fat: 13g; Carbohydrates: 20g; Fiber: 3g; Protein: 12g; Calcium: 201mg; Vitamin D: 0mcg; Vitamin B_{12} : 0µg; Iron: 3mg; Zinc: 2mg

Mushroom French Onion Soup

MAKES 2 SERVINGS • PREP TIME: 10 MINUTES • COOK TIME: 20 MINUTES

Ingredients

- 1 tablespoon olive oil
- 1 tablespoon unsalted butter
- 1 cup thinly sliced onion (1 medium)
- 1 cup sliced fresh mushrooms
- 3 cups mushroom or vegetable broth
- 2 teaspoons dried thyme
- Kosher salt
- Freshly ground black pepper
- 2 slices provolone cheese
- 2 slices whole-grain bread

Directions:

Step 1.
Heat the oil and butter in an 8-quart stockpot over medium-low heat. Once the butter is melted, add the onion and cook gently, stirring occasionally, for 5 minutes, or until translucent.

Step 2.
Add the mushrooms and cook for an additional 3 minutes.

Step 3.
Add the broth and thyme, and season with salt and pepper.

Step 4.
Increase the heat to high and bring the soup to a boil. Once the soup is boiling, reduce the heat to low and simmer for 5 minutes.

Step 5.
Place a slice of provolone on top of each piece of bread and toast in a toaster oven or under the oven broiler until the cheese is melted.

Step 6.
Divide the soup between 2 bowls and place a piece of toasted bread on top of each. Serve immediately.

Substitute: If you don't have any bread, substitute with croutons or skip the bread altogether. Instead of provolone cheese, try Swiss or Gruyère. Top the bread with nut cheese or nutritional yeast to make this recipe dairy-free.

PER SERVING: Calories: 361; Total fat: 26g; Carbohydrates: 21g; Fiber: 3g; Protein: 12g; Calcium: 253mg; Vitamin D: 0mcg; Vitamin B_{12} : 0μg; Iron: 1mg; Zinc: 2mg

Vegan Corn Chowder

MAKES 4 SERVINGS • PREP TIME: 10 MINUTES • COOK TIME: 20 MINUTES

Ingredients

- 2 tablespoons grapeseed oil
- ½ cup diced red onion
- 3 cups frozen corn kernels
- 1 red bell pepper, cored, seeded, and diced
- 2 jalapeño peppers, seeded and diced (optional)
- 1 tablespoon ground cumin
- 1 tablespoon chili powder
- 4 cups plain unsweetened soy milk (or plain unsweetened milk of choice)
- 2 cups cooked black beans (or 2 [15-ounce] cans, drained and rinsed)
- Kosher salt

Directions:

Step 1.
Heat the oil in a 12-quart stockpot over medium heat. Once the oil is shiny, add the onion and cook for 4 minutes, stirring often, or until the onion is translucent.

Step 2.
Add the corn, bell pepper, jalapeño (if using), cumin, and chili powder. Cook for 5 minutes, or until the corn is thawed. Add the soy milk and increase the heat to high. Once the mixture is boiling, reduce the heat to low and simmer for 10 minutes.

Step 3.
Transfer the soup in batches to a blender and blend for 30 seconds or until the soup is smooth and creamy. Transfer the blended soup to a large bowl and add the black beans. Season to taste with salt. Serve.

Tip: If you include dairy in your lifestyle, substitute cow's milk for the soy milk in this recipe. Other plant milk varieties also work; just make sure they're unsweetened and plain (not vanilla flavored).

Storage: Store leftover soup in an airtight container in the refrigerator for up to 1 week or freeze for up to 3 months.

PER SERVING: Calories: 431; Total fat: 13g; Carbohydrates: 67g; Fiber: 13g; Protein: 19g; Calcium: 344mg; Vitamin D: 3mcg; Vitamin B_{12}: 2µg; Iron: 5mg; Zinc: 3mg

High-Protein Lentil Soup

MAKES 4 SERVINGS • PREP TIME: 10 MINUTES • COOK TIME: 25 MINUTES

Ingredients

- 2 tablespoons grapeseed oil
- 1 small onion, diced (½ cup)
- 1 large carrot, diced (1 cup)
- 2 celery stalks, diced (1 cup)
- ½ teaspoon kosher salt
- ¼ teaspoon freshly ground black pepper
- 3 garlic cloves, chopped
- 1 tablespoon ground cumin
- 2 cups dried lentils
- 1 (28-ounce) can crushed tomatoes
- 4 cups vegetable broth
- 2 cups water, or more as needed

Directions:

Step 1.

Heat the oil in a 12-quart stockpot over medium heat. Once the oil is shiny, add the onion, carrot, celery, salt, and pepper and cook for 5 minutes or until the onion is translucent. Add the garlic and cumin and cook for an additional 1 minute.

Step 2.

Add the lentils, tomatoes, broth, and 2 cups water. Cover the pot and increase the heat to high. Once the mixture is boiling, reduce the heat to medium-low and simmer for 15 minutes, or until the lentils are softened. Add an additional cup of water as needed if you want the soup to be thinner.

Step 3.

Adjust the salt and pepper to taste. Serve.

Protein swaps: If you want to switch things up, try making this soup with green or yellow split peas. Like lentils, dried peas belong to the legume family, which is a sustainable source of plant-based protein.

Storage: Store leftover soup in an airtight container in the refrigerator for up to 1 week or freeze for up to 3 months. You may need to add more water before reheating the soup.

PER SERVING: Calories: 510; Total fat: 9g; Carbohydrates: 87g; Fiber: 15g; Protein: 28g; Calcium: 101mg; Vitamin D: 0mcg; Vitamin B_{12}: 0µg; Iron: 11mg; Zinc: 4mg

Broccoli Cheese Soup with Croutons

MAKES 4 SERVINGS • PREP TIME: 20 MINUTES • COOK TIME: 30 MINUTES

Ingredients

FOR THE CROUTONS
- 2 cups torn leftover bread, in 2-inch pieces
- 1 tablespoon olive oil
- 1 teaspoon dried thyme
- Kosher salt
- Freshly ground black pepper

FOR THE SOUP
- 2 tablespoons unsalted butter
- 1 small onion, diced (½ cup)
- 1 large carrot, diced (1 cup)
- 4 garlic cloves, chopped
- 1 tablespoon dried thyme
- ¼ cup all-purpose flour
- 2 cups vegetable broth
- 2 cups milk
- 2 cups chopped broccoli florets
- 8 ounces cheddar cheese, freshly grated (about 2 cups)

Directions:

Step 1.
To make the croutons: Preheat the oven to 375°F.

Step 2.
In a medium bowl, toss together the bread, olive oil, and thyme. Season with salt and pepper to taste and spread the bread cubes on an unlined baking sheet. Bake for 15 minutes or until golden. Remove from the oven and set aside to cool.

Step 3.
To make the soup: Heat the butter in a 12-quart stockpot over medium heat. Once the butter is melted, add the onion and carrot and cook for 5 minutes or until the onion is translucent. Add the garlic and thyme and cook for an additional 1 minute.

Step 4.
Add the flour and cook for 3 minutes, stirring often. Add the broth, milk, and broccoli and increase the heat to high. Once the mixture is boiling, reduce the heat to low and simmer for 5 minutes or until the broccoli is softened.

Step 5.
Add the cheese and simmer until it is melted. Divide the soup among 4 bowls and top each bowl with a few croutons.

Storage: Store leftover soup in an airtight container in the refrigerator for up to 1 week or freeze for up to 3 months. Leftover croutons can be stored in an airtight container at room temperature for 3 days.

Tip: Packaged shredded cheese usually contains an ingredient to prevent it from sticking together. Because of this, commercially shredded cheese may not mix into the soup as well as freshly grated. If you don't mind the texture change, use it here to make preparation easier.

PER SERVING: Calories: 513; Total fat: 33g; Carbohydrates: 32g; Fiber: 2g; Protein: 23g; Calcium: 592mg; Vitamin D: 1mcg; Vitamin B_{12} : 1µg; Iron: 2mg; Zinc: 3mg

Irish-Inspired Potato Stew

MAKES 4 SERVINGS • PREP TIME: 10 MINUTES • COOK TIME: 55 MINUTES

Ingredients

- 2 tablespoons grapeseed oil, or more as needed
- 1 medium onion, diced
- 4 cups peeled and chopped potatoes
- 2 cups diced carrots
- 3 garlic cloves, chopped
- 1 tablespoon dried thyme
- 4 cups vegetable broth
- 1 cup dried split peas, rinsed
- Kosher salt
- Freshly ground black pepper
- 4 scallions, both white and green parts, chopped

Directions:

Step 1.
Heat the 2 tablespoons oil in a 12-quart stockpot over medium heat. Once the oil is shiny, add the onion and cook for 4 minutes, stirring often, or until the onion is translucent.

Step 2.
Add the potatoes, carrots, garlic, and thyme and cook for 10 minutes, stirring occasionally, and adding more oil as needed to prevent sticking.

Step 3.
Add the broth and dried peas, cover, and increase the heat to high. Cook until the peas are softened, about 35 minutes. Season the stew to taste with salt and pepper. Transfer the stew to bowls and garnish with the scallions.

Storage: Store leftover stew in an airtight container in the refrigerator for up to 1 week or freeze for up to 3 months.

Make it easier: Swap in canned beans or canned lentils for the split peas. Since canned beans and lentils are already cooked, you can save about 30 minutes when you use them in this recipe.

PER SERVING: Calories: 404; Total fat: 8g; Carbohydrates: 70g; Fiber: 18g; Protein: 16g; Calcium: 78mg; Vitamin D: 0mcg; Vitamin B_{12} : 0µg; Iron: 4mg; Zinc: 3mg

Vegan Gumbo

MAKES 2 SERVINGS • PREP TIME: 10 MINUTES • COOK TIME: 20 MINUTES

Ingredients

- 2 tablespoons grapeseed oil
- ½ medium onion, diced (1 cup)
- 1 cup diced celery
- 1 green bell pepper, cored, seeded, and diced
- 1 tablespoon Cajun seasoning
- 3 cups vegetable broth
- 1 (15-ounce) can red kidney beans, drained and rinsed
- 1 cup chopped fresh collard greens

Directions:

Step 1.

Heat the oil in a 12-quart stockpot over medium heat. Once the oil is shiny, add the onion, celery, and green pepper and cook for 5 minutes or until the onion is translucent.

Step 2.

Add the Cajun seasoning and cook for an additional 1 minute.

Step 3.

Add the broth, kidney beans, and collard greens. Bring the soup to a simmer and cook for 10 minutes.

Storage: Store leftover soup in an airtight container in the refrigerator for up to 1 week or freeze for up to 3 months.

Protein swaps: Instead of kidney beans, substitute tofu, tempeh, or cannellini beans. You can also use sliced plant-based sausages if you happen to have them on hand.

PER SERVING: Calories: 357; Total fat: 15g; Carbohydrates: 45g; Fiber: 13g; Protein: 13g; Calcium: 111mg; Vitamin D: 0mcg; Vitamin B_{12} : 0µg; Iron: 5mg; Zinc: 2mg

Pumpkin and Black Bean Chili

MAKES 4 SERVINGS • PREP TIME: 10 MINUTES • COOK TIME: 20 MINUTES

Ingredients

- 2 tablespoons grapeseed oil, or more as needed

- 1 small onion, diced
- 1 large carrot, diced
- 1 cup frozen corn kernels
- 2 tablespoons chili powder
- 1 tablespoon ground cumin
- ½ teaspoon kosher salt
- ¼ teaspoon freshly ground black pepper
- 1 (28-ounce) can crushed tomatoes
- 1 (15-ounce) can pumpkin puree
- 1 cup vegetable broth
- 2 (15-ounce) cans black beans, drained and rinsed
- 2½ cups chopped fresh kale (1 pound)

Directions:

Step 1.

Heat the 2 tablespoons oil in a 12-quart stockpot over medium heat. Once the oil is shiny, add the onion and cook for 4 minutes, stirring often, or until the onion is translucent.

Step 2.

Add the carrot, corn, chili powder, cumin, and salt and pepper and cook for 5 minutes. Add more oil as needed to prevent sticking.

Step 3.

Add the crushed tomatoes, pumpkin puree, vegetable broth, black beans, and chopped kale and cook for 10 minutes, or until the chili is hot and the carrot is softened. Serve.

Storage: Store leftover chili in an airtight container in the refrigerator for up to 1 week or freeze for up to 3 months.

Tip: Instead of black beans, try substituting kidney beans, pinto beans, lentils, or tempeh. If you can't find canned pumpkin, substitute 2 cups mashed sweet potatoes or pureed butternut squash.

PER SERVING: Calories: 429; Total fat: 11g; Carbohydrates: 72g; Fiber: 26g; Protein: 21g; Calcium: 337mg; Vitamin D: 0mcg; Vitamin B_{12}: 0μg; Iron: 9mg; Zinc: 3mg

Peanut Stew

MAKES 2 SERVINGS • PREP TIME: 10 MINUTES • COOK TIME: 25 MINUTES

Ingredients

- 1 tablespoon grapeseed oil
- 1 small onion, diced
- 1 medium sweet potato, peeled and chopped (1¼ cups)

- 1 (1-inch) piece of fresh ginger, peeled and grated
- 2 garlic cloves, chopped
- ¼ teaspoon cayenne (optional)
- 2 cups vegetable broth
- 2 tablespoons tomato paste
- ⅓ cup peanut butter
- ½ cup chopped fresh collard greens or kale

Directions:

Step 1.

Heat the oil in a 12-quart stockpot, Dutch oven, or deep skillet over medium heat. Add the onion, sweet potato, ginger, garlic, and cayenne (if using), and cook for 5 minutes or until the onion is translucent.

Step 2.

Add the broth, tomato paste, and peanut butter and bring to a simmer.

Step 3.

Add the collard greens or kale and simmer for 15 minutes, or until the sweet potato is softened. Serve.

Storage: Store leftover soup in an airtight container in the refrigerator for up to 1 week or freeze for up to 3 months.

Tip: If you have a peanut allergy, try making this stew with sunflower seed butter. Add canned beans or cooked tofu if you want to bump up the protein.

PER SERVING: Calories: 418; Total fat: 29g; Carbohydrates: 34g; Fiber: 6g; Protein: 12g; Calcium: 81mg; Vitamin D: 0mcg; Vitamin B_{12}: 0µg; Iron: 2mg; Zinc: 1mg

Green Goddess Cucumber-Avocado Sandwiches

MAKES 2 SANDWICHES • PREP TIME: 5 MINUTES

Ingredients

- ½ cup plain Greek yogurt
- 1 medium avocado, peeled, pitted, and mashed
- ¾ cup chopped fresh parsley
- 2 tablespoons fresh lemon juice
- 1 garlic clove, minced
- ¼ teaspoon kosher salt
- ⅛ teaspoon freshly ground black pepper
- 4 slices whole-grain bread
- ½ English cucumber, peeled and sliced

- ½ cup fresh baby spinach

Directions:

Step 1.

Put the yogurt, avocado, parsley, lemon juice, garlic, salt, and pepper in a food processor and process for 1 minute, or until creamy, pausing to scrape down the sides with a spatula as needed.

Step 2.

Spread the yogurt mixture on each slice of bread. Divide the cucumber slices and spinach between 2 slices of bread. Place the other slices, spread-side down, on top of the vegetables. Cut the sandwiches in half, if desired. Serve.

Mix it up: Instead of parsley, make this sandwich spread with a mix of fresh basil and spinach to change the flavors. For a South of the Border twist, use fresh cilantro and lime juice.

PER SERVING (1 SANDWICH): Calories: 373; Total fat: 20g; Carbohydrates: 41g; Fiber: 13g; Protein: 14g; Calcium: 185mg; Vitamin D: 0mcg; Vitamin B_{12}: 0μg; Iron: 3mg; Zinc: 2mg

Cranberry and Chickpea Salad Sandwiches

MAKES 2 SANDWICHES • PREP TIME: 10 MINUTES

Ingredients

- 1 (15-ounce) can chickpeas, drained and rinsed
- ⅓ cup plain Greek yogurt
- ⅓ cup dried cranberries
- ¼ cup fresh basil leaves, torn (or 1 tablespoon dried)
- 1 tablespoon apple cider vinegar
- ¼ teaspoon kosher salt
- ⅛ teaspoon freshly ground black pepper
- 4 slices whole-grain bread, toasted if desired

Directions:

Step 1.

In a small bowl, stir together the chickpeas and yogurt. Use a fork or potato masher to mash the chickpeas slightly.

Step 2.

Add the cranberries, basil, vinegar, salt, and pepper, and stir to mix thoroughly.

Step 3.

Spread the chickpea mixture on 2 slices of bread.

Step 4.

Top with the remaining bread slices. Serve.

Mix it up: Use raisins instead of cranberries and add 1 tablespoon of curry powder to give these sandwiches a new flavor profile. You can also use fresh cilantro or mint instead of basil.

PER SERVING (1 SANDWICH): Calories: 427; Total fat: 7g; Carbohydrates: 75g; Fiber: 14g; Protein: 19g; Calcium: 166mg; Vitamin D: 0mcg; Vitamin B_{12} : 0µg; Iron: 5mg; Zinc: 3mg

Spicy Peanut-Tofu Lettuce Wraps

MAKES 2 WRAPS • PREP TIME: 5 MINUTES • COOK TIME: 10 MINUTES

Ingredients

- 1 tablespoon coconut oil (or grapeseed oil)
- ½ (14-ounce) block extra-firm tofu, drained, pressed (see Tip), and cubed
- ¼ teaspoon kosher salt
- ½ cup cooked brown rice
- 1½ cups Spicy Peanut Sauce or store-bought sauce
- 2 large romaine lettuce leaves
- ¼ cup chopped fresh cilantro
- Chopped peanuts (optional)

Directions:

Step 1.

Heat the coconut oil in a large skillet over medium heat. Once melted, arrange the tofu in a single layer in the skillet, sprinkle with the salt, and cook for 5 minutes, or until the bottom of the tofu is golden brown and easily separates from the pan.

Step 2.

Flip the tofu and cook for 3 minutes more, or until the other side is golden brown and easily separates from the pan. Transfer to a large bowl.

Step 3.

Add the brown rice and spicy peanut sauce to the bowl. Then, divide the tofu mixture between the lettuce leaves. Add the cilantro and peanuts (if using). Serve immediately.

Protein swaps: If you want to avoid cooking the tofu, try swapping in shelled edamame, which you can steam in the microwave before mixing with the brown rice and spicy peanut sauce. This is an excellent option if you don't have a stovetop or hot plate.

Tip: To cook perfect brown rice, bring 6 cups of water and a dash of kosher salt to a boil over high heat in a large saucepan and add 1 cup rinsed brown rice. Reduce to medium-low and boil, uncovered, for 30 minutes. Drain, cover, and set aside for 10 to 15 minutes. This makes about 4 cups cooked rice.

PER SERVING (1 WRAP): Calories: 532; Total fat: 35g; Carbohydrates: 30g; Fiber: 4g; Protein: 29g; Calcium: 389mg; Vitamin D: 0mcg; Vitamin B_{12}: 0μg; Iron: 4mg; Zinc: 4mg

Curried Egg Salad Sandwiches

MAKES 2 SANDWICHES • PREP TIME: 10 MINUTES

Ingredients

- 4 large hard-boiled eggs, chopped
- ½ cup plain Greek yogurt
- 3 scallions, both white and green parts, chopped
- 1 celery stalk, diced
- 1 tablespoon grainy mustard
- 2 teaspoons curry powder
- ¼ teaspoon kosher salt
- ¼ teaspoon freshly ground black pepper
- 4 slices whole-grain bread

Directions:

Step 1.

In a medium bowl, mix the eggs, yogurt, scallions, celery, mustard, curry powder, salt, and pepper until well combined.

Step 2.

Spread the egg salad on 2 slices of bread and top with the remaining slices of bread. Cut the sandwiches in half, if desired. Serve.

Tip: To make perfect hard-boiled eggs, place a medium saucepan filled three-fourths full of lightly salted water on high heat and bring to a boil. Gently lower the eggs into it, reduce heat to keep a medium boil, and cook for 7 minutes (for a soft center) or 8 minutes (for a harder center). As soon as they're done, transfer eggs to ice water to get them to stop cooking.

Protein swap: Use cubed tofu, chickpeas, or white beans to make this recipe egg-free. For a vegan variation, use one of these plant-based protein sources along with plain dairy-free yogurt.

PER SERVING: Calories: 338; Total fat: 14g; Carbohydrates: 30g; Fiber: 6g; Protein: 23g; Calcium: 219mg; Vitamin D: 2mcg; Vitamin B_{12}: 1μg; Iron: 4mg; Zinc: 3mg

Smoky Lentil and Portobello Mushroom Wraps

MAKES 2 WRAPS • PREP TIME: 5 MINUTES • COOK TIME: 10 MINUTES

Ingredients

- ¼ cup grapeseed oil, plus some to coat skillet
- 1 tablespoon tahini
- 1 tablespoon apple cider vinegar
- 2 teaspoons smoked paprika
- 1 teaspoon ground cumin
- ¼ teaspoon cayenne (optional)
- ¼ teaspoon kosher salt
- 2 fresh portobello mushroom caps, cut into 2-inch pieces
- 1 cup cooked lentils
- 2 leaves fresh kale, thick stems cut out and leafy parts chopped
- 2 large corn tortillas

Directions:

Step 1.

In a large bowl, whisk together the ¼ cup oil, the tahini, vinegar, smoked paprika, cumin, cayenne (if using), and salt.

Step 2.

Add the mushrooms and toss with your hands until they're evenly coated with the sauce.

Step 3.

Pour a little oil into a large skillet and preheat it over medium heat.

Step 4.

Transfer the mushrooms to the skillet and cook for 5 minutes, stirring occasionally, or until the mushrooms soften and darken in color. Add a little more oil as needed to prevent the mushrooms from sticking.

Step 5.

Add the lentils and kale and cook for 3 minutes, or until the kale is wilted.

Step 6.

Wrap the tortillas in a paper towel or a clean cloth and microwave on high for 20 seconds. Lay the tortillas on a clean work surface and spread the mushroom mixture on them. Fold up the sides and then roll up each tortilla to form a wrap. Serve immediately.

Substitute: Tahini is a ground sesame seed paste that's often found either near the peanut butter or in the Middle Eastern section of the grocery store. If you can't find it, substitute creamy peanut butter or almond butter (see Lemon Tahini recipe).

PER SERVING: Calories: 608; Total fat: 36g; Carbohydrates: 58g; Fiber: 14g; Protein: 19g; Calcium: 232mg; Vitamin D: 0mcg; Vitamin B_{12} : 0µg; Iron: 8mg; Zinc: 3mg

Lemon Basil and Smashed White Bean Sandwiches

MAKES 2 SANDWICHES • PREP TIME: 10 MINUTES

Ingredients

- 1 (15-ounce) can cannellini beans, drained and rinsed
- ⅓ cup fresh basil leaves
- 2 garlic cloves, minced
- 2 tablespoons fresh lemon juice
- 1 tablespoon olive oil, or more as needed
- ¼ teaspoon kosher salt
- ⅛ teaspoon freshly ground black pepper
- 4 slices whole-grain bread
- ½ cup fresh baby spinach or torn lettuce
- ½ ripe medium tomato, sliced

Directions:

Step 1.

Put the cannellini beans, basil, garlic, lemon juice, 1 tablespoon olive oil, salt, and pepper in a food processor. Process until smooth, pausing to scrape down the sides with a spatula as needed. If it isn't mixing, gradually add more oil and process again.

Step 2.

Spread the bean mixture on each slice of bread. Divide the spinach or lettuce and the tomato between 2 of the bread slices. Place the other slices of bread, spread-side down, on top of the tomato. Cut the sandwiches in half, if desired. Serve.

Mix it up: There are endless opportunities for changing the flavors of these white bean sandwiches. Instead of fresh basil, try spinach, parsley, or cilantro. You can also add ground spices. Try curry powder, Cajun seasoning, za'atar, or a dash of cayenne.

PER SERVING: Calories: 377; Total fat: 10g; Carbohydrates: 55g; Fiber: 13g; Protein: 19g; Calcium: 110 mg; Vitamin D: 0mcg; Vitamin B_{12} : 0µg; Iron: 4mg; Zinc: 2mg

Loaded Carrot Dogs

MAKES 2 SERVINGS • PREP TIME: 10 MINUTES, PLUS 30 MINUTES TO MARINATE COOK TIME: 20 MINUTES

Ingredients

- Kosher salt
- 2 medium carrots, peeled and cut to match bun length
- 2 tablespoons soy sauce
- 2 tablespoons apple cider vinegar
- 1 teaspoon smoked paprika
- 1 teaspoon maple syrup
- 2 hot dog buns

OPTIONAL FOR SERVING

- 2 tablespoons ketchup
- 2 tablespoons mustard
- ¼ cup diced onion
- ¼ cup sliced jalapeño pepper

Directions:

Step 1.

Place a medium saucepan filled three-fourths full of lightly salted water on high heat and bring to a boil. Add the carrots, carefully using tongs, and boil until the vegetables are fork-tender, about 15 minutes.

Step 2.

While the carrots are boiling, place the soy sauce, vinegar, smoked paprika, and maple syrup in a sealable medium plastic bag, seal the bag, and shake it until the ingredients are mixed.

Step 3.

Add the hot boiled carrots to the bag, seal again, and let the carrots marinate for at least 30 minutes or in the refrigerator overnight.

Step 4.

Preheat a grill pan or outdoor grill and grill the carrots until hot and lightly marked with grill marks, rotating every couple of minutes to evenly cook the vegetable.

Step 5.

Place the carrots inside the hot dog buns and top with the ketchup, mustard, onion, and jalapeño, if desired.

Mix it up: Load up these carrot dogs just like you would a regular hot dog. In addition to the toppings here, you can try topping them with Red Cabbage and Cilantro Slaw , Pumpkin and Black Bean Chili , sauerkraut, or relish.

PER SERVING: Calories: 165; Total fat: 2g; Carbohydrates: 31g; Fiber: 3g; Protein: 6g; Calcium: 105mg; Vitamin D: 0mcg; Vitamin B_{12} : 0µg; Iron: 2mg; Zinc: 1mg

Mediterranean Falafel Pitas

MAKES 2 PITAS • PREP TIME: 15 MINUTES • COOK TIME: 30 MINUTES

Ingredients

FOR THE FALAFEL
- ¼ cup grapeseed oil
- 1 (15-ounce) can chickpeas, drained and rinsed well
- ½ cup whole wheat flour
- ½ cup diced red onion
- ½ cup shredded carrot
- 1 tablespoon ground cumin
- ¼ teaspoon kosher salt
- ⅛ teaspoon freshly ground black pepper

FOR THE PITAS
- 2 pita flatbreads, 1 inch trimmed off tops of each, warmed if desired
- ½ cup sliced cucumber
- ½ cup sliced tomato
- ½ cup sliced red onion
- ¼ cup tahini
- 2 tablespoons fresh lemon juice

Directions:

Step 1.
To make the falafel: Preheat the oven to 375°F and pour the oil onto a rimmed baking sheet. Tilt the baking sheet until the surface is evenly coated with the oil.

Step 2.
Put the chickpeas, flour, red onion, carrot, cumin, salt, and pepper in a food processor and process for 1 minute or until a thick paste forms.

Step 3.
Use your hands to roll the mixture into balls, about 2 tablespoons for each ball, and transfer the balls to the baking sheet, arranging them in a single layer.

Step 4.
Bake the falafels for 30 minutes, carefully flipping them halfway through; be careful because the falafels and oil on the baking sheet are very hot. Let the falafels cool enough to handle, about 15 minutes.

Step 5.
To make the pitas: Open the pockets of the pita breads and place half the baked falafels into each. Stuff each pita bread with some cucumber, tomato, red onion, tahini, and lemon juice. Serve.

Tip: If you don't have access to an oven, try pan-frying the falafels in a skillet. Coat the skillet with about ¼ inch of oil and spread the falafels in a single layer in the pan. Cook until the bottoms turn golden brown and then flip and cook on the other side, about 12 minutes in total.

PER SERVING (1 PITA): Calories: 850; Total fat: 48g; Carbohydrates: 89g; Fiber: 18g; Protein: 24g; Calcium: 274mg; Vitamin D: 0mcg; Vitamin B_{12} : 0µg; Iron: 10mg; Zinc: 5mg

Roasted Sweet Potato and Hummus Sandwiches

MAKES 2 SANDWICHES • PREP TIME: 10 MINUTES • COOK TIME: 15 MINUTES

Ingredients

- 1 small sweet potato, peeled and sliced thinly lengthwise
- 1 tablespoon grapeseed oil
- ¼ teaspoon kosher salt
- ⅛ teaspoon freshly ground black pepper
- 4 slices whole-grain bread, toasted if desired
- ½ cup Classic Hummus or store-bought hummus
- 1 small avocado, peeled, pitted, and sliced
- ½ cup fresh baby spinach
- ¼ cup fresh basil

Directions:

Step 1.
Preheat the oven or a toaster oven to 400°F. Line a baking sheet with parchment.

Step 2.
Spread the sweet potato slices in a single layer on the baking sheet, brush the slices with the oil, and sprinkle them with the salt and pepper. Roast the sweet potato for 15 minutes, or until golden and softened. Let the sweet potato slices cool enough to be able to handle, about 15 minutes.

Step 3.
Lay the bread slices on a flat surface. Spread 2 tablespoons of hummus on each piece of bread.

Step 4.
Evenly lay the sweet potato slices, the avocado, spinach, and basil on 2 of the bread slices.

Step 5.
Top with the remaining bread slices, hummus-side down. Cut the sandwiches in half, if desired. Serve.

Mix it up: Use any type of sandwich spread for this recipe. Instead of hummus, try White Bean Sandwich Spread or the yogurt-based Green Goddess spread.

PER SERVING (1 SANDWICH): Calories: 547; Total fat: 30g; Carbohydrates: 60g; Fiber: 17g; Protein: 15g; Calcium: 131mg; Vitamin D: 0mcg; Vitamin B_{12}: 0µg; Iron: 3mg; Zinc: 2mg

Vegan Banh Mi Sandwiches

MAKES 2 SANDWICHES • PREP TIME: 10 MINUTES, PLUS 30 MINUTES TO MARINATE • COOK TIME: 10 MINUTES

Ingredients

- 1 tablespoon grapeseed oil, plus some to grease skillet
- 1 tablespoon soy sauce
- 1 teaspoon honey or maple syrup
- 1 (1-inch) piece of fresh ginger, grated (or 1¼ teaspoons ground ginger)
- ½ (14-ounce) block extra-firm tofu, drained, pressed, and sliced into 4 pieces
- 2 (6-inch) baguettes, cut into 4 slices (or 2 sandwich rolls, halved)
- 1 cup pickled vegetables (such as pickled carrots and jalapeños)
- ¼ cup mayonnaise (regular or vegan)
- ¼ cup fresh cilantro

Directions:

Step 1.

In a small bowl, whisk together the 1 tablespoon oil, the soy sauce, honey, and ginger and transfer the mixture to a sealable medium plastic or reusable silicone bag.

Step 2.

Add the tofu pieces to the bag, seal it, and marinate for at least 30 minutes or in the refrigerator overnight.

Step 3.

Lightly oil a skillet and preheat it over medium heat.

Step 4.

Arrange the tofu in a single layer in the skillet and cook for 4 minutes, or until the pieces easily separate from the pan. Flip them over and cook for an additional 4 minutes, or until they again easily separate from the pan.

Step 5.

Divide the tofu between 2 of the baguette slices and top with the pickled vegetables, mayonnaise, and cilantro. Place the remaining baguette slices on top. Serve.

Tip: Instead of using store-bought pickles, make your own by using a favorite recipe or try Quick Pickled Carrots and Vegetables .

PER SERVING (1 SANDWICH): Calories: 400; Total fat: 23g; Carbohydrates: 31g; Fiber:

3g; Protein: 17g; Calcium: 287mg; Vitamin D: 0mcg; Vitamin B_{12} : 0µg; Iron: 4mg; Zinc: 2mg

Chickpea and Coconut Curry Wraps

MAKES 2 WRAPS • PREP TIME: 5 MINUTES • COOK TIME: 20 MINUTES

Ingredients

- 1 tablespoon grapeseed oil
- ½ cup diced onion
- 1 tablespoon curry powder
- ¼ teaspoon garlic powder
- ¼ teaspoon ground ginger
- ¼ teaspoon kosher salt
- ¼ teaspoon freshly ground black pepper
- 2 cups chopped broccoli florets
- 1 (15-ounce) can chickpeas, drained and rinsed
- 1 (1Step 3.5-ounce) can unsweetened coconut milk
- 2 large flour tortillas

Directions:

Step 1.

Heat the oil in a large skillet over medium heat. Once the oil is shiny, add the onion and cook for 4 minutes or until translucent.

Step 2.

Add the curry powder, garlic powder, ground ginger, salt, and pepper, and cook for 1 minute more.

Step 3.

Add the broccoli and chickpeas and cook for 3 minutes, or until the broccoli turns bright green.

Step 4.

Add the coconut milk and simmer for 10 minutes or until the curry is thickened.

Step 5.

Wrap the tortillas in a paper towel or a clean cloth and microwave them for 20 seconds. Lay them on a clean work surface.

Step 6.

Divide the curry between the tortillas, fold up the sides of the tortillas, and roll them up to form the wraps. Serve immediately.

Protein swaps: Instead of chickpeas, try simmering dried lentils in the curry sauce for about 15 minutes, or until they're tender. Cubed tofu also works well as a plant-based protein source for this recipe.

PER SERVING (1 WRAP): Calories: 780; Total fat: 53g; Carbohydrates: 64g; Fiber: 15g; Protein: 21g; Calcium: 199mg; Vitamin D: 0mcg; Vitamin B_{12} : 0µg; Iron: 12mg; Zinc: 4mg

Crispy Eggplant BLTs

MAKES 2 SANDWICHES • PREP TIME: 10 MINUTES, PLUS 30 MINUTES SALTING TIME COOK TIME: 30 MINUTES

Ingredients

- ½ small eggplant, peeled and cut into thin slices (see Tip)
- 1 to 2 tablespoons kosher salt
- 1 tablespoon grapeseed oil
- 1 tablespoon soy sauce
- 2 teaspoons smoked paprika
- 2 teaspoons maple syrup
- ½ teaspoon freshly ground black pepper
- ¼ cup mayonnaise (regular or vegan)
- 4 slices whole wheat bread
- 4 lettuce leaves
- 1 ripe medium tomato, sliced

Directions:

Step 1.

Place the eggplant slices in a colander and sprinkle generously with the salt. Wait 30 minutes, rinse, and then pat dry.

Step 2.

Preheat the oven to 300°F. Line a baking sheet with parchment.

Step 3.

In a medium bowl, whisk together the oil, soy sauce, smoked paprika, maple syrup, and black pepper.

Step 4.

Add the eggplant slices and toss until evenly coated with the sauce. Arrange the eggplant on the baking sheet in a single layer and bake for 30 minutes or until dry and crispy. Remove the eggplant from the oven and allow to cool for 5 minutes before assembling the sandwiches.

Step 5.

Spread the mayonnaise on 2 slices of bread. Arrange the eggplant pieces, lettuce, and tomato on top. Place the remaining bread slices on top and cut the sandwiches in half, if desired. Serve.

Tip: To cut the eggplant, first slice off the stem end and peel. Then cut it in half lengthwise. Slice one of the halves again and use a knife to cut ⅛-inch-thick strips along the flat edge of the eggplant. Save the remaining half for other uses.

PER SERVING: Calories: 385; Total fat: 19g; Carbohydrates: 43g; Fiber: 10g; Protein: 13g; Calcium: 160mg; Vitamin D: 0mcg; Vitamin B_{12}: 0µg; Iron: 3mg; Zinc: 2mg

Vegan Sushi Burritos

MAKES 2 BURRITOS • PREP TIME: 10 MINUTES • COOK TIME: 3 MINUTES

Ingredients

- 1 cup frozen shelled edamame
- ½ cup cooked brown rice (see Tip)
- ½ cup shredded carrot
- 1 tablespoon soy sauce
- 1 teaspoon ground ginger
- 1 teaspoon maple syrup
- ½ teaspoon garlic powder
- 2 sheets nori seaweed

Directions:

Step 1.
Heat the edamame in the microwave in a small bowl according to the package instructions, then transfer it to a large bowl.

Step 2.
Add the rice, carrot, soy sauce, ginger, maple syrup, and garlic powder.

Step 3.
Use a damp cloth or paper towel to wipe the nori sheets until they become soft and flexible.

Step 4.
Lay the nori sheets on a flat surface. Spoon the edamame mixture into the center of each nori sheet, then fold in the sides and roll up to form burritos. Serve immediately.

Substitute: If you can't find nori, try using rice paper (spring roll wrappers) instead. You can also skip the wrap altogether and turn this recipe into a sushi bowl.

PER SERVING (PER WRAP): Calories: 180; Total fat: 5g; Carbohydrates: 26g; Fiber: 6g; Protein: 11g; Calcium: 72mg; Vitamin D: 0mcg; Vitamin B_{12} : 0µg; Iron: 2mg; Zinc: 2mg

Veggie and White Bean Pesto Melt

MAKES 4 SANDWICHES • PREP TIME: 5 MINUTES • COOK TIME: 10 MINUTES

Ingredients

- 1 (15-ounce) can white beans (such as cannellini or Great Northern), drained and rinsed
- 1 cup Carrot-Top Pesto or store-bought pesto
- 1 tablespoon unsalted butter
- 8 slices whole-grain bread
- 1 ripe medium tomato, sliced
- 1 cup shredded mozzarella cheese
- Grapeseed oil or nonstick cooking spray

Directions:

Step 1.

In a medium bowl, mash the beans with a potato masher or a fork until they form a lumpy paste.

Step 2.

Add the pesto and stir to combine.

Step 3.

Spread a little butter on each piece of bread. Turn 4 of the pieces over so they are butter-side down and spread the bean mixture on the other side. Top the bean mixture with the tomato and mozzarella cheese. Place the remaining bread slices, butter-side up, on top of the cheese.

Step 4.

Pour a little oil into a large skillet or grill pan and heat over medium heat. When the skillet is hot, place the sandwiches in it in a single layer (cook in batches, if needed). Cook for 5 minutes, or until the bread is golden. Carefully flip the sandwiches and cook for an additional 5 minutes, or until the other side is golden and the cheese is melted. Serve.

Mix it up: Don't have any mozzarella? Try these sandwiches with cheddar, pepper jack, or goat cheese instead—any type of cheese that melts when heated. You can also look for plant-based butter and cheese alternatives to make this recipe vegan.

PER SERVING (1 SANDWICH): Calories: 657; Total fat: 47g; Carbohydrates: 40g; Fiber: 9g; Protein: 25g; Calcium: 387mg; Vitamin D: 0mcg; Vitamin B_{12} : 1µg; Iron: 4mg; Zinc: 3mg

Chili-Lime Tempeh Burritos

MAKES 2 WRAPS • PREP TIME: 10 MINUTES • COOK TIME: 10 MINUTES

Ingredients

- 2 tablespoons grapeseed oil
- ¼ cup diced red onion
- 1 (8-ounce) block firm tempeh, crumbled
- 1 cup frozen corn kernels

- 1 tablespoon fresh lime juice
- 2 teaspoons chili powder
- 2 teaspoons ground cumin
- ½ cup chopped fresh cilantro
- 2 large flour tortillas, warmed
- ½ cup Spicy Blender Salsa or store-bought salsa
- ½ cup Chunky Guacamole or store-bought guacamole

Directions:

Step 1.

Heat the oil in a medium skillet over medium heat.

Step 2.

Once the oil is shiny, add the onion and cook for 4 minutes or until translucent.

Step 3.

Add the tempeh, corn, lime juice, chili powder, and cumin, and cook for 3 minutes, stirring occasionally, or until tempeh is warmed.

Step 4.

Add the cilantro and turn off the heat.

Step 5.

Lay a tortilla on a flat surface and spoon half the tempeh mixture into the center. Top with some salsa and guacamole. Fold over each side and then roll up the tortilla to form the burrito. Repeat with the remaining tortilla.

Step 6.

Serve immediately, or place them in an airtight container and refrigerate for up to 1 week or freeze for up to 3 months.

Protein swaps: If you have an allergy to soy or just can't find tempeh in your area, swap in a can of black beans or pinto beans. Drain and rinse the canned beans before adding them to the skillet with the other ingredients.

PER SERVING (1 WRAP): Calories: 642; Total fat: 38g; Carbohydrates: 59g; Fiber: 10g; Protein: 29g; Calcium: 229mg; Vitamin D: 0mcg; Vitamin B_{12} : 0µg; Iron: 7mg; Zinc: 3mg

Freezer-Friendly Bean Burgers

MAKES 4 SERVINGS • PREP TIME: 10 MINUTES • COOK TIME: 10 MINUTES

Ingredients

- 2 (15-ounce) cans black beans, drained and rinsed
- 1 cup cooked brown rice (see Tip)
- 1 large carrot, shredded and squeezed dry

- ¼ cup diced onion
- ¼ cup chopped fresh cilantro
- 1 large egg, lightly beaten
- 1 tablespoon tomato paste
- 1 tablespoon chili powder
- ½ teaspoon kosher salt
- ¼ teaspoon freshly ground black pepper
- Grapeseed oil or nonstick cooking spray
- 4 hamburger buns

Directions:

Step 1.

In a large bowl, mash the black beans with a fork or a potato masher.

Step 2.

Add the rice, carrot, onion, cilantro, egg, tomato paste, chili powder, salt, and pepper and stir until combined.

Step 3.

Use your hands to form 4 patties. Press until the patties stick together. (If patties aren't as firm as you'd like, chill them on a plate in the refrigerator for 30 minutes.)

Step 4.

Pour a little oil into a large skillet and heat over medium-high heat. When the skillet is hot, arrange the patties in it in a single layer (cook in batches, if needed) and cook for 5 minutes, or until the bottom turns golden brown. Flip the patties and cook for an additional 5 minutes, or until both sides are golden and the patties are cooked through. Serve on hamburger buns.

Step 5.

To freeze, wrap each patty in aluminum foil or parchment paper and store in a freezer-safe bag. To reheat, unwrap a burger patty and microwave on a plate for 3 minutes, or until hot. You can also reheat patties in a greased skillet.

Mix it up: Use this recipe as a basic formula to make all types of bean burgers. Swap in chickpeas for the black beans and add 1 tablespoon of curry powder to give these patties some Indian flare.

PER SERVING: Calories: 375; Total fat: 4g; Carbohydrates: 67g; Fiber: 15g; Protein: 18g; Calcium: 134mg; Vitamin D: 0mcg; Vitamin B_{12} : 0µg; Iron: 5mg; Zinc: 2mg

Lentil Sloppy Joes

MAKES 4 SERVINGS • PREP TIME: 5 MINUTES • COOK TIME: 15 MINUTES

Ingredients

- 1 tablespoon grapeseed oil
- ¼ cup diced onion
- 3 garlic cloves, minced
- 2 cups cooked lentils
- 1 (15-ounce) can tomato sauce
- 1 tablespoon soy sauce
- 1 teaspoon chili powder
- 1 teaspoon ground cumin
- ¼ teaspoon cayenne (optional)
- 4 rolls or hamburger buns

Directions:

Step 1.

Heat the oil in a large skillet over medium heat.

Step 2.

Once the oil is shiny, add the onion and cook for 4 minutes or until translucent.

Step 3.

Add the garlic and cook for 1 additional minute.

Step 4.

Add the lentils, tomato sauce, soy sauce, chili powder, cumin, and cayenne (if using). Simmer the mixture for 10 minutes, or until it is warmed through and thickened.

Step 5.

Divide the lentil mixture among the rolls or hamburger buns and serve.

Storage: Store leftover sloppy joe filling in an airtight container in the refrigerator for up to 1 week.

Protein swaps: Instead of lentils, try this recipe with crumbled tempeh or canned beans. Just make sure you drain and rinse the beans before stirring them into the skillet with the other ingredients.

PER SERVING: Calories: 308; Total fat: 6g; Carbohydrates: 51g; Fiber: 11g; Protein: 15g; Calcium: 142mg; Vitamin D: 0mcg; Vitamin B_{12} : 0μg; Iron: 7mg; Zinc: 2mg

Mushroom Cheesesteaks

MAKES 2 SANDWICHES • PREP TIME: 5 MINUTES • COOK TIME: 15 MINUTES

Ingredients

- 1 tablespoon grapeseed oil
- ½ sweet onion, thinly sliced
- 2 fresh portobello mushroom caps, cut into ¼-inch slices

- ½ teaspoon crushed dried rosemary (optional)
- ¼ teaspoon cayenne (optional)
- ¼ teaspoon kosher salt
- ⅛ teaspoon freshly ground black pepper
- 2 hoagie rolls, halved
- 2 slices provolone cheese

Directions:

Step 1.

Preheat the oven or toaster oven to 400°F. Line a baking sheet with parchment.

Step 2.

Heat the grapeseed oil in a large skillet over medium heat.

Step 3.

Once the oil is shiny, add the onion and cook for 4 minutes or until translucent.

Step 4.

Add the mushrooms, rosemary (if using), cayenne (if using), salt, and pepper and cook for 2 minutes, or until the mushrooms begin to darken in color.

Step 5.

Arrange the hoagie rolls cut-side up on the baking sheet. Evenly divide the mushroom mixture between 2 of the hoagie halves and top with the provolone cheese.

Step 6.

Bake until the cheese is melted, about 5 minutes.

Step 7.

Place the hoagie halves on top of the mushroom cheese halves and serve.

Substitute: If you can't find portobello mushroom caps, swap in 2¼ cups sliced cremini, shiitake, or baby bella mushrooms. Instead of provolone cheese, use Swiss.

PER SERVING (1 SANDWICH): Calories: 320; Total fat: 16g; Carbohydrates: 31g; Fiber: 3g; Protein: 14g; Calcium: 304mg; Vitamin D: 0mcg; Vitamin B_{12} : 1μg; Iron: 2mg; Zinc: 2mg

Tempeh Reubens

MAKES 2 SANDWICHES • PREP TIME: 5 MINUTES • COOK TIME: 15 MINUTES

Ingredients

- 4 teaspoons unsalted butter
- 4 slices rye bread
- 1 tablespoon grapeseed oil, plus more to grease skillet
- 1 tablespoon soy sauce

- 1 teaspoon smoked paprika
- 2 teaspoons apple cider vinegar
- 1 (8-ounce) block firm tempeh, sliced into 4 pieces
- ¼ cup Russian dressing
- ½ cup sauerkraut
- 2 slices Swiss cheese (optional)

Directions:

Step 1.

Spread the butter on one side of each piece of bread.

Step 2.

In a small bowl, whisk together the 1 tablespoon oil, the soy sauce, smoked paprika, and vinegar.

Step 3.

Lightly grease a large skillet and place it over medium heat.

Step 4.

Brush the spiced oil onto the tempeh pieces and arrange them in the skillet in a single layer. Cook for 6 minutes, flipping halfway through, or until the tempeh is warmed through. Transfer the cooked tempeh to a plate or bowl and set aside.

Step 5.

Place the bread, butter-side down, in a single layer in the skillet (cook in batches, if needed) and cook until golden, about 3 minutes. Remove the bread from the skillet to a clean work surface, placing the slices with the golden cooked side down.

Step 6.

Spread the Russian dressing on the top of each piece of bread.

Step 7.

Divide the fried tempeh, sauerkraut, and Swiss cheese (if using) between 2 of the slices. Place the remaining pieces of bread, dressing-side down, on top of the tempeh mixture. Serve immediately.

Tip: To make this recipe vegan, use vegan butter or coconut oil instead of butter and omit the Swiss cheese. If you don't have Swiss cheese but still want the melty texture it provides, try a couple slices of provolone instead.

PER SERVING (1 SANDWICH): Calories: 600; Total fat: 36g; Carbohydrates: 47g; Fiber: 5g; Protein: 27g; Calcium: 185mg; Vitamin D: 0mcg; Vitamin B_{12} : 0μg; Iron: 6mg; Zinc: 2mg

Buffalo Tofu Sandwiches

MAKES 2 SANDWICHES • PREP TIME: 5 MINUTES, PLUS 30 MINUTES TO MARINATE COOK TIME: 10 MINUTES

Ingredients

- ½ (14-ounce) block firm tofu, drained, pressed, and sliced into 4 pieces
- ¼ cup buffalo-style hot sauce, plus additional for serving
- Grapeseed oil or nonstick cooking spray
- ¼ cup crumbled blue cheese (optional)
- 2 sandwich rolls, halved
- ½ cup fresh baby spinach or torn lettuce of choice
- ¼ cup thinly sliced onion

Directions:

Step 1.

Brush the tofu pieces with the hot sauce and place them on a plate or in a container, cover, and allow them to marinate for at least 30 minutes or in the refrigerator overnight.

Step 2.

Lightly oil a large skillet and preheat it over medium heat.

Step 3.

Arrange the tofu in a single layer in the skillet and cook the tofu pieces for 4 minutes, or until they easily separate from the pan. Flip them over and cook for an additional 4 minutes, or until the other side easily separates. Remove the skillet from the heat.

Step 4.

Brush the tofu with more hot sauce and sprinkle with the blue cheese (if using).

Step 5.

Divide the tofu between the sandwich rolls and top with the spinach or lettuce and onion. Serve.

Mix it up: If you're looking for a way to make these sandwiches more portable, try turning them into wraps. Just use 2 warmed flour tortillas instead of buns for a satisfying weekday lunch.

PER SERVING: Calories: 209; Total fat: 8g; Carbohydrates: 25g; Fiber: 2g; Protein: 11g; Calcium: 193mg; Vitamin D: 0mcg; Vitamin B_{12} : 0μg; Iron: 3mg; Zinc: 1mg

Cucumber-Mango Salad

MAKES 2 SERVINGS • PREP TIME: 10 MINUTES

Ingredients

- 1 ripe mango, pitted and cut into 1-inch-wide strips
- 1 cucumber, halved lengthwise, seeded, and cut into 4-inch-long and 1-inch-wide strips
- ⅓ cup chopped fresh cilantro

- 1 jalapeño pepper, sliced
- 1 teaspoon grated lime zest
- 1 tablespoon fresh lime juice
- Kosher salt

Directions:

Step 1.

In a large bowl, toss together the mango, cucumber, cilantro, jalapeño, lime zest, and lime juice until well mixed. Season to taste with salt.

Step 2.

Transfer to 2 plates and serve immediately.

Substitute: Use frozen mango chunks instead of fresh mango, if desired. Thaw them in the refrigerator or in the microwave. Canned mango also works for this recipe. Look for fruit canned in fruit juice (not syrup) and strain the fruit from the canning liquid before using.

PER SERVING: Calories: 125; Total fat: 1g; Carbohydrates: 30g; Fiber: 4g; Protein: 3g; Calcium: 40mg; Vitamin D: 0mcg; Vitamin B_{12}: 0µg; Iron: 1mg; Zinc: 0mg

Thai-Inspired Peanut Salad

MAKES 4 SERVINGS • PREP TIME: 15 MINUTES

Ingredients

- 2½ cups frozen shelled edamame, thawed
- 2 cups shredded red cabbage
- 2 cups chopped fresh baby spinach
- 1 cup shredded carrots
- 1 cup roasted peanuts
- 1½ cups Spicy Peanut Sauce or store-bought sauce
- ⅓ cup chopped fresh cilantro

Directions:

Step 1.

In a large bowl, toss together the thawed edamame, red cabbage, spinach, carrots, roasted peanuts, and peanut sauce until well mixed.

Step 2.

Add the cilantro and lightly toss to mix. Serve.

Storage: Store leftover salad in an airtight container in the refrigerator for up to 1 week.

Make it easier: Look for a bag of coleslaw vegetables to use in place of the cabbage, spinach, and carrots. Doing so will cut your chopping and prep time.

PER SERVING: Calories: 415; Total fat: 23g; Carbohydrates: 33g; Fiber: 12g; Protein: 22g; Calcium: 145mg; Vitamin D: 0mcg; Vitamin B_{12}: 0µg; Iron: 4mg; Zinc: 3mg

Strawberry and Avocado Spinach Salad

MAKES 2 SERVINGS • PREP TIME: 10 MINUTES

Ingredients

- 3 cups fresh baby spinach
- 1 cup sliced fresh strawberries
- 1 medium avocado, peeled, pitted, and diced
- ¾ cup Lemon Tahini Dressing or store-bought dressing
- ¼ cup sunflower seeds, toasted if desired
- ¼ cup chopped fresh basil (optional)

Directions:

Step 1.
In a large bowl, combine the spinach, strawberries, and avocado.

Step 2.
Pour in the dressing and toss gently until the ingredients are evenly coated.

Step 3.
Add the sunflower seeds and basil (if using) and gently toss until just incorporated. Serve immediately.

Protein swaps: Use 1 can of drained and rinsed chickpeas instead of (or in addition to) sunflower seeds for more protein. You can also include chopped almonds or hemp hearts.

PER SERVING: Calories: 432; Total fat: 32g; Carbohydrates: 31g; Fiber: 15g; Protein: 13g; Calcium: 162mg; Vitamin D: 0mcg; Vitamin B_{12}: 0µg; Iron: 4mg; Zinc: 3mg

Red Cabbage and Cilantro Slaw

MAKES 4 TO 8 SERVINGS • PREP TIME: 10 MINUTES

Ingredients

- 3 cups shredded red cabbage
- 1 cup shredded carrots
- 1 cup chopped fresh cilantro
- ¼ cup sunflower or pumpkin seeds (optional; see Tip)
- 2 scallions, both white and green parts, chopped

- ¼ cup olive oil
- 2 tablespoons apple cider vinegar
- 1 teaspoon honey
- Kosher salt
- Freshly ground black pepper

Directions:

Step 1.

In a large bowl, mix the red cabbage, carrots, cilantro, sunflower or pumpkin seeds (if using), and scallions.

Step 2.

In a small bowl, whisk together the olive oil, vinegar, and honey. Season to taste with salt and pepper. Pour the dressing over the cabbage mixture and toss until the vegetables are evenly coated. Serve immediately.

Storage: Store leftover salad in an airtight container in the refrigerator for up to 1 week.

Tip: To toast the sunflower or pumpkin seeds, preheat the oven (or a toaster oven) to 350°F and spread the seeds on a baking sheet. Bake for 5 minutes, or until the seeds are golden and very aromatic.

PER SERVING (AS SIDE): Calories: 162; Total fat: 14g; Carbohydrates: 10g; Fiber: 3g; Protein: 1g; Calcium: 48mg; Vitamin D: 0mcg; Vitamin B_{12}: 0μg; Iron: 1mg; Zinc: 0mg

Make-Ahead Kale Salad

MAKES 2 TO 4 SERVINGS • PREP TIME: 5 MINUTES

Ingredients

- 1 pound fresh kale, chopped
- 1 (15-ounce) can chickpeas, drained and rinsed
- ⅓ cup chopped almonds
- ⅓ cup dried cranberries
- ¼ cup Apple Cider Vinaigrette or store-bought dressing

Directions:

Step 1.

In a large bowl, massage the kale for 3 minutes, or until tender.

Step 2.

Add the chickpeas, almonds, cranberries, and vinaigrette and toss to combine. Serve.

Storage: Store leftover salad in an airtight container in the refrigerator for up to 1 week.

Substitute: If you're allergic to nuts, try swapping in hemp hearts, sunflower seeds, or pumpkin seeds for the almonds. You can also use raisins or halved grapes instead of the dried cranberries if desired.

PER SERVING (AS ENTRÉE): Calories: 660; Total fat: 33g; Carbohydrates: 77g; Fiber: 21g; Protein: 23g; Calcium: 443mg; Vitamin D: 0mcg; Vitamin B_{12} : 0µg; Iron: 8mg; Zinc: 4mg

Vegan Greek Salad with Tofu Feta
MAKES 4 SERVINGS • PREP TIME: 10 MINUTES

Ingredients

- 2 tablespoons olive oil
- 1 tablespoon fresh lemon juice
- 1 teaspoon dried oregano
- ⅛ teaspoon kosher salt
- ⅛ teaspoon freshly ground black pepper
- ½ cup Tofu Feta or store-bought tofu
- 1 pint cherry tomatoes, halved
- 1 English cucumber, chopped
- 1 green bell pepper, cored, seeded, and chopped
- ½ cup sliced red onion
- ½ cup pitted Kalamata olives

Directions:
Step 1.
In a large bowl, whisk together the olive oil, lemon juice, oregano, salt, and pepper until well blended.

Step 2.
Add the tofu feta, tomatoes, cucumber, green pepper, onion, and olives to the dressing and gently stir until the ingredients are evenly coated. Serve immediately.

Storage: Store leftover salad in an airtight container in the refrigerator for up to 3 days.

Substitute: Use other types of black olives if you can't find Kalamata. Substitute regular feta cheese if you include dairy products in your diet and want to make this recipe easier to prepare.

PER SERVING: Calories: 184; Total fat: 14g; Carbohydrates: 10g; Fiber: 3g; Protein: 8g; Calcium: 211mg; Vitamin D: 0mcg; Vitamin B_{12} : 0µg; Iron: 2mg; Zinc: 1mg

Caprese Pasta Salad

MAKES 2 SERVINGS • PREP TIME: 5 MINUTES • COOK TIME: 20 MINUTES

Ingredients

- Kosher salt
- 4 ounces dried whole wheat penne (or other pasta of choice)
- ¼ cup olive oil
- 2 tablespoons fresh lemon juice
- 1 teaspoon dried oregano
- ⅛ teaspoon freshly ground black pepper
- 1 cup cherry tomatoes, halved
- 4 ounces fresh mozzarella pearls (small balls, or cut into ½-inch pieces)
- ¾ cup fresh basil leaves (torn, if large)

Directions:

Step 1.

Bring an 8-quart stockpot filled three-fourths full of water and 1 teaspoon salt to a boil over high heat. Pour in the penne and cook for 11 minutes, stirring occasionally, or according to package instructions, until al dente.

Step 2.

Drain the pasta, reserving about 2 tablespoons of the cooking liquid in the pot.

Step 3.

Return the pasta to the pot over medium heat and add the olive oil, lemon juice, oregano, ⅛ teaspoon salt, and the pepper. Toss to mix.

Step 4.

Add the cherry tomatoes, mozzarella, and fresh basil leaves and stir. Cook until the mozzarella begins to melt and the liquid is absorbed, about 3 minutes. Adjust the seasonings, if needed.

Step 5.

You can serve the pasta hot, allow it to cool to room temperature, or chill and serve cold.

Storage: Store leftover salad in an airtight container in the refrigerator for up to 4 days.

Make it easier: A classic Caprese salad doesn't usually have pasta, so leave it out if you want to try out a more authentic version of this dish. During the summer months, I also love to swap in sliced heirloom tomatoes.

PER SERVING: Calories: 624; Total fat: 40g; Carbohydrates: 48g; Fiber: 6g; Protein: 21g; Calcium: 326mg; Vitamin D: 0mcg; Vitamin B_{12} : 1μg; Iron: 3mg; Zinc: 3mg

Creamy Greek Yogurt Potato Salad

MAKES 4 SERVINGS • PREP TIME: 5 MINUTES • COOK TIME: 10 MINUTES

Ingredients

- 3 medium russet or Yukon Gold potatoes, chopped into 1-inch pieces
- 1 cup plain Greek yogurt
- ¼ cup mustard, such as Dijon
- 2 celery stalks, diced, including leaves
- ½ cup chopped red onion
- Kosher salt
- Freshly ground black pepper
- Smoked paprika (optional)

Directions:

Step 1.

Place the potatoes in a 12-quart stockpot and cover with cold water. Bring to a boil over high heat, reduce the heat to medium-low, and simmer for 6 minutes, or until the potatoes are pierced easily with a fork. Drain the water, return the potatoes to the stockpot, and allow them to cool enough to handle.

Step 2.

While the potatoes are cooling, in a medium bowl, stir together the yogurt and mustard.

Step 3.

Add the celery and red onion and stir to combine.

Step 4.

Pour the yogurt mixture over the cooled potatoes and gently toss until thoroughly mixed. Season to taste with salt and pepper.

Step 5.

Transfer the salad to a serving dish, top with a sprinkling of smoked paprika (if using), and serve.

Storage: Store leftover salad in an airtight container in the refrigerator for up to 5 days.

Substitute: Looking for a way to make this classic creamy salad vegan and dairy-free? There are a lot of delicious plant-based yogurts available these days. You can also try vegan mayonnaise. Look for both in the refrigerated section near the tofu.

PER SERVING: Calories: 272; Total fat: 3g; Carbohydrates: 55g; Fiber: 5g; Protein: 9g; Calcium: 127mg; Vitamin D: 0mcg; Vitamin B_{12}: 0µg; Iron: 3mg; Zinc: 1mg

Edamame Mason Jar Salad

MAKES 2 SERVINGS • PREP TIME: 10 MINUTES

Ingredients

- 2 tablespoons toasted sesame oil
- 1 tablespoon soy sauce
- 1 tablespoon rice vinegar
- 1 teaspoon honey or maple syrup (optional)
- ½ cup shredded red cabbage
- ½ cup shredded carrot
- 1 small bell pepper, cored, seeded, and diced
- 1 cup frozen shelled edamame, thawed
- 1 cup cooked brown rice (see Tip)

Directions:

Step 1.

In a medium bowl, whisk together the sesame oil, soy sauce, rice vinegar, and honey until well blended.

Step 2.

Divide the dressing between two 1-pint jars with lids (about 3 tablespoons per jar).

Step 3.

In the same bowl as you used for the dressing, toss together the red cabbage, carrot, and bell pepper until well mixed, then evenly divide the mixture between the jars.

Step 4.

Evenly divide the edamame and cooked brown rice between the jars. To serve, pour the contents of each jar onto a plate.

Protein swaps: If you want to bulk this up, try adding cooked tofu. You could also add crunchy roasted peanuts to the top of the jar and use Spicy Peanut Sauce instead of the dressing in the recipe.

Storage: Refrigerate the salads for up to 1 week.

PER SERVING: Calories: 364; Total fat: 19g; Carbohydrates: 39g; Fiber: 8g; Protein: 12g; Calcium: 88mg; Vitamin D: 0mcg; Vitamin B_{12} : 0μg; Iron: 3mg; Zinc: 2mg

Vegan Caesar Salad

MAKES 2 SERVINGS • PREP TIME: 10 MINUTES

Ingredients

FOR THE DRESSING

- ½ cup silken tofu

- ¼ cup nutritional yeast
- 3 tablespoons olive oil
- 3 tablespoons apple cider vinegar
- 5 pitted Kalamata olives
- 1 teaspoon dried chives
- ¼ teaspoon garlic powder
- ⅛ teaspoon kosher salt
- ⅛ teaspoon freshly ground black pepper

FOR THE SALAD
- 1 head romaine lettuce, chopped
- 1 cup Whole-Grain Croutons or store-bought croutons
- ½ cup pitted Kalamata olives, chopped

Directions:

Step 1.
To make the dressing: Place the tofu, nutritional yeast, olive oil, vinegar, whole olives, chives, garlic powder, salt, and pepper in a blender or food processor and pulse until smooth. If the dressing is too thick, add a tablespoon of water and pulse again.

Step 2.
To make the salad: In a large bowl, toss the romaine lettuce and dressing until the lettuce is evenly coated.

Step 3.
Add the croutons and chopped olives to the bowl. Serve immediately.

Storage: If you have leftovers, keep the croutons separate and store them in an airtight container at room temperature. Store the salad in an airtight container in the refrigerator for up to 1 week.

Substitute: If you can't find silken tofu or aren't able to tolerate soy, substitute with plain yogurt or a plain dairy-free yogurt alternative. Substitute Parmesan cheese for nutritional yeast if you include dairy. Substitute black olives or capers for the kalamata olives.

PER SERVING: Calories: 476; Total fat: 28g; Carbohydrates: 42g; Fiber: 11g; Protein: 17g; Calcium: 252mg; Vitamin D: 0mcg; Vitamin B_{12} : 0μg; Iron: 7mg; Zinc: 3mg

Sun-Dried Tomato and Farro Salad

MAKES 4 SERVINGS • PREP TIME: 15 MINUTES • COOK TIME: 15 MINUTES

Ingredients

- 1½ cups water

- Kosher salt
- ½ cup farro
- 2 cups fresh baby spinach
- 1 (15-ounce) can chickpeas, drained and rinsed
- ½ cup chopped sun-dried tomatoes
- 2 tablespoons olive oil
- 1 tablespoon fresh lemon juice
- ½ teaspoon garlic powder
- Freshly ground black pepper

Directions:

Step 1.

In an 8-quart stockpot, bring the water and ¼ teaspoon salt to a boil and add the farro. Cook the farro for 15 minutes, or until the desired consistency is reached. (You can cook longer for a softer texture.) Drain the excess water and transfer the cooked farro to a large bowl.

Step 2.

Add the spinach, chickpeas, sun-dried tomatoes, olive oil, lemon juice, and garlic powder to the farro and toss until well combined. Season with salt and pepper. Serve immediately.

Storage: Store leftover salad in an airtight container in the refrigerator for up to 1 week.

Tip: Look for microwavable farro, which you can often steam right in the package to save on dishes you'll have to clean up. This version is great to save time or if you don't have access to a hot plate or stovetop.

PER SERVING: Calories: 524; Total fat: 18g; Carbohydrates: 77g; Fiber: 18g; Protein: 20g; Calcium: 120mg; Vitamin D: 0mcg; Vitamin B12: 0µg; Iron: 7mg; Zinc: 4mg

Cranberry, Walnut, and Brussels Sprouts Salad

MAKES 2 SERVINGS • PREP TIME: 20 MINUTES • COOK TIME: 1 HOUR

Ingredients

- 3 cups water
- Kosher salt
- ⅓ cup pearled barley
- 2 tablespoons grapeseed oil
- 3 cups shredded Brussels sprouts
- Freshly ground black pepper
- ½ cup walnut halves and pieces, toasted if desired
- ¼ cup dried cranberries
- 1 tablespoon apple cider vinegar

Directions:

Step 1.

In an 8-quart stockpot, bring the water and ¼ teaspoon salt to a boil over high heat. Add the barley, reduce the heat to low, and cook for 55 minutes, or until the grain is chewy and tender. Drain the excess cooking water if needed and fluff with a fork. Transfer the barley to a large bowl.

Step 2.

In a large skillet, heat the oil over medium heat. Add the Brussels sprouts and cook for 4 minutes, stirring occasionally, or until the sprouts are lightly browned. Season with salt and pepper and transfer to the bowl with the barley.

Step 3.

Add the walnuts, cranberries, and vinegar and toss to combine. Serve.

Storage: Store leftover salad in an airtight container in the refrigerator for up to 1 week.

Mix it up: Substitute any grain for the barley, such as farro or brown rice. Use crumbled feta or goat cheese instead of walnuts for a nut-free version. Try it with creamy Lemon Tahini Dressing .

PER SERVING: Calories: 533; Total fat: 34g; Carbohydrates: 54g; Fiber: 13g; Protein: 12g; Calcium: 96mg; Vitamin D: 0mcg; Vitamin B_{12} : 0µg; Iron: 4mg; Zinc: 2mg

Harvest Butternut Squash and Quinoa Salad

MAKES 4 SERVINGS • PREP TIME: 10 MINUTES • COOK TIME: 20 MINUTES

Ingredients

- 1 cup water
- Kosher salt
- ⅓ cup quinoa, rinsed
- 1 medium butternut squash, peeled, seeded, and cubed
- 1 tablespoon grapeseed oil
- 1 tablespoon maple syrup
- Freshly ground black pepper
- 1 pound fresh kale, chopped
- ¼ cup chopped pecans
- ¼ cup dried cranberries
- ¼ cup Apple Cider Vinaigrette or store-bought dressing

Directions:

Step 1.

Preheat the oven to 450°F. Line a baking sheet with parchment.

Step 2.

In an 8-quart stockpot, bring the water and ⅛ teaspoon salt to a boil. Add the quinoa, reduce the heat to medium-low, and cook for 15 minutes or until the quinoa is tender. Drain any excess cooking liquid if needed and fluff with a fork.

Step 3.

While the quinoa is cooking, in a large bowl, toss together the squash, oil, maple syrup, and salt and pepper to taste until the vegetables are well coated. Spread the cubes on the baking sheet. Bake for 20 minutes or until the squash is tender and golden.

Step 4.

When the squash is almost done baking, place the kale in a large bowl and massage it with your hands for 5 minutes, or until tender.

Step 5.

Add the quinoa, pecans, cranberries, and squash.

Step 6.

Pour in the dressing and gently toss until the ingredients are evenly coated. Serve warm.

Storage: Store leftover salad in an airtight container in the refrigerator for up to 1 week.

Substitute: Any type of hearty winter squash works for this recipe. Try substituting acorn or kabocha varieties. Cubed sweet potato will also be delicious if you want to add more sweetness. You can also use toasted pumpkin seeds instead of the pecans.

PER SERVING: Calories: 363; Total fat: 20g; Carbohydrates: 44g; Fiber: 8g; Protein: 9g; Calcium: 237mg; Vitamin D: 0mcg; Vitamin B$_{12}$: 0µg; Iron: 3mg; Zinc: 2mg

Sesame-Ginger Soba Noodle Salad

MAKES 2 SERVINGS • PREP TIME: 5 MINUTES • COOK TIME: 20 MINUTES

Ingredients

- 1 (**Step 2.**67-ounce) bundle soba noodles (from multi-bundle package)
- 1 tablespoon coconut oil
- 2 cups chopped fresh broccoli florets
- 1 cup frozen shelled edamame
- ¼ cup chopped scallions, both white and green parts
- ¼ cup Sesame Ginger Dressing or store-bought dressing

Directions:

Step 1.

In an 8-quart stockpot, bring about 6 cups of water to a boil and add the soba noodles. Boil for 6 minutes or according to the package instructions. Drain and transfer to a large bowl.

Step 2.

Heat the coconut oil in the same pot over medium heat. Once the oil is melted, add the broccoli and cook for 5 minutes, or until it turns bright green.

Step 3.

Add the frozen edamame and scallions and cook for another 5 minutes, or until the edamame is warmed through.

Step 4.

Add the cooked noodles and dressing, stirring to combine all the ingredients, then immediately remove from the heat.

Storage: Store leftover salad in an airtight container in the refrigerator for up to 1 week.

Tip: Substitute with udon or rice noodles if you can't find soba. Change the vegetables and use bok choy, snap peas, or mushrooms instead of broccoli. For a plant-based protein swap, use tofu instead of edamame.

PER SERVING: Calories: 315; Total fat: 31g; Carbohydrates: 46g; Fiber: 7g; Protein: 18g; Calcium: 127mg; Vitamin D: 0mcg; Vitamin B_{12} : 0μg; Iron: 4mg; Zinc: 2mg

Chili-Lime Taco Salad

MAKES 2 SERVINGS • PREP TIME: 5 MINUTES • COOK TIME: 15 MINUTES

Ingredients

- 2 tablespoons grapeseed oil
- ¼ cup diced red onion
- 1 (15-ounce) can black beans, drained and rinsed
- 1 tablespoon fresh lime juice
- 2 teaspoons chili powder
- 2 teaspoons ground cumin
- ½ cup chopped fresh cilantro
- 2 cups chopped romaine lettuce
- 2 large store-bought tortilla bowls (optional)
- ½ cup Spicy Blender Salsa or store-bought salsa
- ½ cup Chunky Guacamole or store-bought guacamole

Directions:

Step 1.

Heat the oil in a medium skillet over medium heat. When the oil is hot, add the onion and cook for 4 minutes or until translucent.

Step 2.

Add the beans, lime juice, chili powder, and cumin, and cook for 3 minutes or until beans are warmed through.

Step 3.

Add the cilantro and remove the skillet from the heat.

Step 4.

Divide the lettuce between the tortilla bowls. Divide the bean mixture between the bowls and top with the salsa and guacamole. Serve.

Protein swaps: Instead of black beans, use pinto beans, crumbled tempeh, or cubed tofu. You can also add scrambled eggs to turn this into a flavor-packed breakfast salad.

Tip: You can make your own tortilla bowls if you have time and a 12-cup muffin tin. Preheat the oven to 375°F and microwave 2 large corn tortillas for 20 seconds to make them more flexible (or heat in a skillet). Turn the muffin tin upside down and nestle a tortilla in the space between 4 cups and shape the tortilla to create a bowl. Repeat with the other tortilla. Bake for 15 minutes, or until the tortillas are golden and crispy, then cool on a rack.

PER SERVING: Calories: 571; Total fat: 27g; Carbohydrates: 70g; Fiber: 20g; Protein: 19g; Calcium: 172mg; Vitamin D: 0mcg; Vitamin B_{12}: 0µg; Iron: 7mg; Zinc: 3mg

Zucchini Pasta Primavera

MAKES 2 SERVINGS • PREP TIME: 10 MINUTES • COOK TIME: 10 MINUTES

Ingredients

- 2 tablespoons grapeseed oil
- 1 yellow summer squash, diced
- 1 cup broccoli florets
- ½ cup frozen green peas
- Kosher salt
- Freshly ground black pepper
- ½ cup milk (or plain unsweetened soy milk)
- ½ cup shredded Parmesan cheese
- 1 tablespoon fresh lemon juice
- 2½ cups zucchini noodles
- Torn basil leaves (optional)

Directions:

Step 1.

Heat the oil in a large skillet over medium-low heat. Once the oil shimmers, add the squash, broccoli, and peas. Season with salt and pepper and cook for 4 minutes or until the vegetables are tender.

Step 2.

Add the milk, cheese, and lemon juice to the skillet and stir until the cheese is melted, about 3 minutes.

Step 3.

Add the zucchini noodles and turn off the heat. Toss until the zucchini noodles are evenly coated with the sauce.

Step 4.

Taste and adjust the seasonings. Serve, sprinkled with basil if desired.

Storage: Store in an airtight container in the refrigerator for up to 3 days.

Substitute: If you don't have soy milk but still want to make this recipe dairy-free, swap in any type of plain, unsweetened, plant-based milk instead. Add a can of chickpeas (drained and rinsed) if you want more protein.

PER SERVING: Calories: 338; Total fat: 23g; Carbohydrates: 22g; Fiber: 5g; Protein: 15g; Calcium: 353mg; Vitamin D: 1mcg; Vitamin B_{12} : 1µg; Iron: 2mg; Zinc: 3mg

15-Minute Cacio e Pepe

MAKES 2 SERVINGS • PREP TIME: 5 MINUTES • COOK TIME: 10 MINUTES

Ingredients

- Kosher salt
- 4 ounces whole wheat spaghetti
- 2 teaspoons olive oil
- 2 garlic cloves, minced
- ½ teaspoon freshly ground black pepper
- ¾ cup grated Pecorino Romano cheese
- Fresh herbs, such as parsley or torn basil leaves (optional)

Directions:

Step 1.

Fill an 8-quart stockpot three-fourths full of water and add ⅛ teaspoon salt. Bring to a boil over high heat. Add the spaghetti and cook for 8 minutes, or until al dente.

Step 2.

Reserve 2 tablespoons of the pasta cooking liquid and then drain the spaghetti.

Step 3.

Reduce the heat to low and return the cooked pasta to the stockpot along with the reserved cooking liquid.

Step 4.

Add the olive oil, garlic, black pepper, and cheese.

Step 5.

Cook for 2 minutes, or until the cheese is melted and the sauce is thickened, stirring constantly.

Step 6.

Taste and season with salt, if needed. Serve with fresh herbs, if desired.

Storage: Store the pasta in an airtight container in the refrigerator for up to 5 days.

Mix it up: Cacio e pepe is traditionally very simple, but that doesn't mean you can't play with the basic recipe and find ways to get more color and flavor. In addition to fresh herbs, try adding vegetables, such as spinach, green peas, kale, or broccoli.

PER SERVING: Calories: 399; Total fat: 16g; Carbohydrates: 49g; Fiber: 5g; Protein: 19g; Calcium: 348mg; Vitamin D: 0mcg; Vitamin B_{12} : 1µg; Iron: 2mg; Zinc: 3mg

One-Pot Pantry Pasta

MAKES 2 SERVINGS • PREP TIME: 10 MINUTES • COOK TIME: 30 MINUTES

Ingredients

- 2 tablespoons grapeseed oil
- ½ cup diced onion
- 1 tablespoon dried basil
- ½ teaspoon garlic powder
- ¼ teaspoon kosher salt
- ¼ teaspoon freshly ground black pepper
- 4 ounces whole wheat penne
- 1 (15-ounce) can crushed tomatoes
- 1 cup water, or more as needed
- 2 cups frozen broccoli florets
- 1 (15-ounce) can chickpeas or white beans, drained and rinsed
- Grated Parmesan cheese or nutritional yeast (optional)

Directions:

Step 1.

Heat the oil in a 12-quart stockpot over medium heat.

Step 2.

Once the oil is shiny, add the onion and cook for 4 minutes, or until translucent.

Step 3.

Add the basil, garlic powder, salt, and pepper and cook for 1 additional minute.

Step 4.

Add the penne, tomatoes, and 1 cup water; add a little more water if needed to fully cover the pasta. Bring the mixture to a boil and cook for 12 minutes, or until most of the liquid is absorbed. Stir occasionally, especially if your pot is not heavy-bottomed, to prevent burning.

Step 5.

Add the broccoli and beans and cook until warmed through and the pasta is tender.

Step 6.

Serve the pasta with Parmesan cheese or nutritional yeast, if desired.

Storage: Store the pasta in an airtight container in the refrigerator for up to 5 days.

Protein swaps: If you don't like beans or have trouble digesting them, try making this recipe with lentils, chopped walnuts, or crumbled tempeh instead. You can also leave out the beans out altogether, if preferred.

PER SERVING: Calories: 601; Total fat: 19g; Carbohydrates: 93g; Fiber: 21g; Protein: 24g; Calcium: 210mg; Vitamin D: 0mcg; Vitamin B_{12} : 0μg; Iron: 8mg; Zinc: 4mg

Vegan Pad Thai

MAKES 2 SERVINGS • PREP TIME: 10 MINUTES • COOK TIME: 15 MINUTES

Ingredients

- 4 ounces rice noodles
- 2 tablespoons coconut oil, or more as needed
- 1¼ cups extra-firm tofu, drained, pressed (see Tip), and cut into 1-inch cubes
- 2 cups chopped broccoli florets
- 1 cup Spicy Peanut Sauce or store-bought sauce

OPTIONAL TOPPINGS

- ½ cup roasted peanuts
- Fresh Thai basil leaves
- Fresh cilantro leaves
- Red pepper flakes
- Lime wedges

Directions:

Step 1.

Place an 8-quart stockpot filled three-fourths full of water over high heat and bring to a boil. Cook the pasta according to the package instructions and set aside.

Step 2.

Heat the 2 tablespoons coconut oil in a large skillet over medium heat.

Step 3.

Once the oil is melted, add the tofu and cook for 7 minutes, or until the tofu easily separates from the pot.

Step 4.

Flip the tofu and cook for an additional 3 minutes, or until the other side easily separates and you can stir the tofu without it sticking to the pot. If the tofu is sticking, cook for another minute or so before stirring. Add more oil if needed to coat the pot.

Step 5.

Add the broccoli and cook for 3 minutes, or until bright green and lightly browned on the edges. Turn off the heat.

Step 6.

Add the cooked rice noodles and the peanut sauce and gently toss until the ingredients are evenly coated.

Step 7.

If the noodles are sticking, add a couple tablespoons of water and toss again.

Step 8.

Divide the pasta between 2 bowls and serve with the peanuts, Thai basil, cilantro, red pepper flakes, and lime wedges if desired.

Storage: Store any leftovers in an airtight container in the refrigerator for up to 3 days.

Tip: Instead of tofu, swap in shelled edamame. If you eat eggs, you can also scramble a couple and stir them into the pasta dish for extra protein.

PER SERVING: Calories: 675; Total fat: 36g; Carbohydrates: 67g; Fiber: 6g; Protein: 24g; Calcium: 257mg; Vitamin D: 0mcg; Vitamin B_{12}: 0µg; Iron: 3mg; Zinc: 4mg

Garlic and Miso Ramen Noodles

MAKES 2 SERVINGS • PREP TIME: 5 MINUTES • COOK TIME: 10 MINUTES

Ingredients

- 2 tablespoons grapeseed oil
- 1 baby bok choy, chopped into 1-inch pieces
- 4 garlic cloves, sliced
- 1 (1-inch) piece of fresh ginger, peeled and grated
- 1 (3-ounce) package ramen noodles, seasoning packet discarded
- 1 tablespoon miso paste

OPTIONAL FOR SERVING

- 2 large fried eggs, kept warm
- 1 scallion, both white and green parts, chopped

Directions:

Step 1.

Heat the oil in a 12-quart stockpot over medium heat.

Step 2.

Add the bok choy, garlic, and ginger and cook for 3 minutes, stirring constantly, or until the bok choy is wilted and the mixture is very aromatic. Transfer the mixture to a plate with a slotted spoon.

Step 3.

Fill the stockpot with water, bring to a boil over high heat, and cook the ramen noodles according to the package instructions.

Step 4.

In a small bowl, whisk the miso paste with 2 tablespoons of the cooking liquid from the noodles.

Step 5.

Drain the noodles and add them to the pot.

Step 6.

Add the cooked bok choy mixture and the miso sauce and toss until the noodles and veggies are evenly coated.

Step 7.

Divide the ramen mixture between 2 bowls and top each with a fried egg and chopped scallion, if using. Serve immediately.

Protein swaps: Instead of a fried egg, serve these ramen noodles with baked tofu or steamed edamame to keep this recipe vegan.

PER SERVING: Calories: 431; Total fat: 23g; Carbohydrates: 48g; Fiber: 4g; Protein: 8g; Calcium: 174mg; Vitamin D: 0mcg; Vitamin B_{12}: 0μg; Iron: 4mg; Zinc: 1mg

Tomato-Basil Orecchiette

MAKES 2 SERVINGS • PREP TIME: 5 MINUTES • COOK TIME: 25 MINUTES

Ingredients

- 2 tablespoons grapeseed oil
- ¼ cup diced onion
- 2 garlic cloves, minced
- ¼ teaspoon kosher salt
- ¼ teaspoon freshly ground black pepper

- 4 ounces orecchiette pasta
- 2 cups water, or as more needed
- 1 pint cherry tomatoes
- 1 cup fresh baby spinach
- 1 (15-ounce) can white beans or chickpeas, drained and rinsed (optional)
- ½ cup shredded Parmesan cheese (optional)
- ½ cup torn fresh basil leaves

Directions:

Step 1.

Heat the oil in a 12-quart stockpot over medium heat.

Step 2.

Once the oil is shiny, add the onion and cook for 4 minutes, or until translucent.

Step 3.

Add the garlic, salt, pepper, pasta, and the 2 cups water and bring to a boil. Add more water if needed to cover the pasta and cook for 10 minutes.

Step 4.

Add the tomatoes, spinach, and beans (if using), and cook for 4 minutes, or until the pasta is al dente and most of the liquid is absorbed. Use a wooden spoon to break open the cherry tomatoes as they cook, if desired. If the pasta cooks before all of the liquid is absorbed, ladle out the excess liquid and discard.

Step 5.

Turn off the heat and add the Parmesan cheese and fresh basil leaves, if using.

Step 6.

Taste and adjust the seasoning. Serve.

Storage: Store the pasta in an airtight container in the refrigerator for up to 5 days.

Substitute: If you don't see orecchiette in the pasta aisle at your local grocery store, try making this recipe with penne, rotini, elbows, or small shells instead. Opt for whole wheat pasta to increase the overall fiber content.

PER SERVING: Calories: 371; Total fat: 15g; Carbohydrates: 51g; Fiber: 4g; Protein: 10g; Calcium: 51mg; Vitamin D: 0mcg; Vitamin B_{12} : 0μg; Iron: 2mg; Zinc: 1mg

Ginger-Turmeric Rice Noodles

MAKES 2 SERVINGS • PREP TIME: 5 MINUTES • COOK TIME: 10 MINUTES

Ingredients

- 1 tablespoon grapeseed oil

- 2 cups chopped fresh kale
- 1 cup frozen shelled edamame
- 1 (2-inch) piece of fresh ginger, peeled and grated
- ¼ teaspoon freshly ground black pepper
- 4 ounces brown rice noodles
- 1 tablespoon soy sauce
- 1 teaspoon ground turmeric
- Fresh Thai basil leaves (optional)

Directions:

Step 1.

Heat the oil in a 12-quart stockpot and add the kale, edamame, ginger, and pepper.

Step 2.

Cook for 3 minutes, or until the kale is wilted and the edamame is thawed. Transfer the mixture to a bowl.

Step 3.

Fill the pot with water and bring to a boil over high heat. Cook the rice noodles according to package instructions, then drain and return the noodles to the pot.

Step 4.

Add the kale mixture, soy sauce, and turmeric and toss to combine. Sprinkle on the basil, if using. Serve immediately.

Storage: Store the pasta in an airtight container in the refrigerator for up to 3 days.

Mix it up: You can use almost any quick-cooking vegetable in place of the kale in this recipe. Try broccoli, cauliflower, or snap peas. There's no need for the vegetables to be fresh because frozen and canned varieties work well, too.

PER SERVING: Calories: 380; Total fat: 11g; Carbohydrates: 56g; Fiber: 6g; Protein: 13g; Calcium: 89mg; Vitamin D: 0mcg; Vitamin B_{12} : 0µg; Iron: 3mg; Zinc: 2mg

Baked Spaghetti Squash Lasagna

MAKES 2 SERVINGS • PREP TIME: 5 MINUTES • COOK TIME: 55 MINUTES

Ingredients

- 1 small spaghetti squash, halved
- 1 tablespoon grapeseed oil
- ¼ teaspoon kosher salt
- ¼ teaspoon freshly ground black pepper
- 1 (15-ounce) can white beans, drained and rinsed

- 3 cups Rosemary and Thyme Red Sauce or store-bought sauce
- 1 cup shredded mozzarella cheese
- 1 teaspoon dried oregano
- Red pepper flakes (optional)

Directions:

Step 1.

Preheat the oven to 450°F.

Step 2.

Place the spaghetti squash halves on a parchment-lined baking sheet, brush the squash with the oil, and sprinkle with the salt and pepper.

Step 3.

Roast the squash for 45 minutes, or until the inside of the squash begins to easily separate from the skin. Leave the oven on.

Step 4.

Remove the squash from the oven and use a fork to loosen the strands in the middle of each half to create 2 bowl shapes.

Step 5.

Place the beans in the squash halves and ladle the red sauce on top.

Step 6.

Sprinkle each with the mozzarella and oregano.

Step 7.

Return the squash to the oven and cook until the cheese is melted, about 10 minutes.

Step 8.

Garnish with red pepper flakes, if desired. Serve immediately.

Storage: Cover the squash halves with plastic or beeswax wrap and refrigerate for up to 5 days.

Make it easier: I like to top the cooked squash with the red sauce, but you can also use your favorite jarred pasta sauce to make the prep a little bit easier.

PER SERVING: Calories: 240; Total fat: 14g; Carbohydrates: 28g; Fiber: 10g; Protein: 4g; Calcium: 180mg; Vitamin D: 0mcg; Vitamin B_{12} : 0µg; Iron: 2mg; Zinc: 0mg

One-Pot Broccoli Mac and Cheese

MAKES 2 SERVINGS • PREP TIME: 5 MINUTES • COOK TIME: 15 MINUTES

Ingredients

- 2½ cups whole milk

- 2 cups chopped broccoli florets
- 4 ounces elbow macaroni (or other short pasta)
- 2 tablespoons unsalted butter
- 1½ cups shredded cheddar cheese
- ¼ teaspoon kosher salt
- ¼ teaspoon freshly ground black pepper

Directions:

Step 1.
Pour the milk into an 8-quart stockpot and bring to a simmer over medium heat.

Step 2.
Add the broccoli and macaroni and cook for 7 minutes, or until the pasta is tender.

Step 3.
Turn off the heat and add the butter, cheese, salt, and pepper.

Step 4.
Mix until the butter and cheese are melted, about 2 minutes. Serve immediately.

Storage: Store in an airtight container and refrigerate for up to 5 days.

Mix it up: Change up the vegetable and type of cheese in this recipe to give it a whole new feel. Try spinach or kale with a blend of Parmesan and mozzarella cheeses.

PER SERVING: Calories: 873; Total fat: 51g; Carbohydrates: 64g; Fiber: 4g; Protein: 40g; Calcium: 975mg; Vitamin D: 35mcg; Vitamin B_{12} : 2μg; Iron: 2mg; Zinc: 5m

Five-Spice Noodles

MAKES 2 SERVINGS • PREP TIME: 5 MINUTES • COOK TIME: 20 MINUTES

Ingredients

- 4 ounces rice noodles
- 2 tablespoons grapeseed oil, or more as needed
- 1¼ cups extra-firm tofu, drained, pressed (see Tip), and cut into 1-inch cubes
- 1 baby bok choy, chopped into 1-inch pieces
- 1 cup chopped broccoli florets
- 1 tablespoon toasted sesame oil (or additional grapeseed oil)
- 1 tablespoon soy sauce or gluten-free tamari
- 1 teaspoon Chinese five-spice powder
- 1 teaspoon maple syrup
- Red pepper flakes (optional)

Directions:

Step 1.

Bring a large saucepan filled three-fourths full of water to a boil over high heat and cook the pasta according to the package instructions. Drain.

Step 2.

Heat the 2 tablespoons grapeseed oil in a large skillet over medium heat. Once the oil is heated, add the tofu and cook for 7 minutes, or until the tofu easily separates from the pan. Flip and cook for an additional 3 minutes, or until the other side easily separates and you can stir the tofu without it sticking. If the tofu is sticking, cook for another minute or so before stirring. Add more oil as needed to coat the pan.

Step 3.

Add the bok choy and broccoli and cook for 3 minutes, or until the vegetables are tender. Turn off the heat.

Step 4.

In a small bowl, whisk together the sesame oil, soy sauce, five-spice powder, and maple syrup until blended. Pour the sauce over the tofu and vegetables.

Step 5.

Add the rice noodles to the skillet and toss until all the ingredients are coated with the sauce. Serve with the red pepper flakes, if desired.

Storage: Store the pasta in an airtight container in the refrigerator for up to 5 days.

Substitute: If you can't find five-spice powder, whip together your own simplified version with 1 tablespoon each of cinnamon and ground fennel, ½ teaspoon ground cloves, and freshly ground black pepper to taste.

PER SERVING: Calories: 530; Total fat: 28g; Carbohydrates: 56g; Fiber: 4g; Protein: 17g; Calcium: 258mg; Vitamin D: 0mcg; Vitamin B_{12} : 0µg; Iron: 3mg; Zinc: 2mg

One-Pot Creamy Vegan Rigatoni

MAKES 2 SERVINGS • PREP TIME: 10 MINUTES • COOK TIME: 30 MINUTES

Ingredients

- Kosher salt
- 4 ounces rigatoni pasta (whole wheat, if desired)
- 2 tablespoons grapeseed oil
- 1 small onion, diced
- 1 teaspoon dried thyme
- 1 teaspoon dried oregano
- 2 cups plain oat milk
- 4 cups chopped fresh kale

- ¼ cup nutritional yeast (optional)
- ¼ teaspoon freshly ground black pepper

Directions:

Step 1.

Fill a 12-quart stockpot three-fourths full of water and add a dash of salt. Bring the water to a boil over high heat and cook the pasta according to the package instructions, or until al dente. Drain and transfer to a bowl.

Step 2.

Reduce the heat to medium and place the pot back on the heat. Add the oil.

Step 3.

Once the oil is shiny, add the onion, thyme, and oregano, and cook for about 5 minutes, stirring often until the onion is translucent.

Step 4.

Add the oat milk and cook, uncovered, for 20 minutes, or until the sauce is thickened and reduced to about half its original volume. Add the kale and cook for 5 minutes, or until wilted. Add the nutritional yeast, ¼ teaspoon salt, and the pepper.

Step 5.

Turn off the heat and add the pasta, tossing until the sauce fully coats the noodles. Serve.

Storage: Store the leftovers in an airtight container in the refrigerator for up to 1 week.

Tip: If you don't have oat milk, try substituting regular cow's milk or cream. To keep this recipe vegan, use almond milk; like oat milk, it has a relatively neutral flavor that's ideal for savory applications.

PER SERVING: Calories: 445; Total fat: 15g; Carbohydrates: 61g; Fiber: 4g; Protein: 17g; Calcium: 277mg; Vitamin D: 115mcg; Vitamin B_{12} : 1μg; Iron: 2mg; Zinc: 2mg

Eggplant Bacon Carbonara

MAKES 2 SERVINGS • PREP TIME: 30 MINUTES • COOK TIME: 40 MINUTES

Ingredients

- ½ medium eggplant, peeled and sliced into thin strips ⅛ inch thick
- Kosher salt
- 1 tablespoon grapeseed oil
- 1 tablespoon soy sauce
- 2 teaspoons smoked paprika
- 2 teaspoons maple syrup
- ½ teaspoon freshly ground black pepper
- 2 large eggs

- ¼ cup grated Parmesan cheese
- ¼ cup grated Pecorino Romano (or additional Parmesan)
- 4 ounces whole wheat spaghetti
- Freshly ground black pepper

Directions:

Step 1.

Place the eggplant slices in a colander and sprinkle generously with about 1 teaspoon salt. Wait for 30 minutes, rinse, and then pat the eggplant dry.

Step 2.

Preheat the oven to 300°F. Line a baking sheet with parchment.

Step 3.

In a medium bowl, whisk the oil, soy sauce, smoked paprika, maple syrup, and black pepper until well blended.

Step 4.

Add the eggplant to the sauce, toss until evenly coated, and then place the slices on the baking sheet in a single layer.

Step 5.

Bake the eggplant for 40 minutes, or until dry and crispy. Let cool for 15 minutes, then chop into bite-size pieces. Let cool for at least 15 minutes.

Step 6.

Beat the eggs in a medium bowl. Add the Parmesan and Pecorino Romano, stirring to combine.

Step 7.

Fill a large saucepan three-fourths full of water and add a dash of salt. Bring the water to a boil over high heat and cook the spaghetti according to the package instructions until al dente, about 15 minutes. Reserve 1 cup of the cooking liquid, then drain the pasta and put it back into the saucepan.

Step 8.

Add the eggplant and the egg-cheese mixture to the pasta. Toss together and gradually add some of the reserved cooking liquid if you want the sauce to be creamier.

Step 9.

Taste and season with salt and pepper, if needed. Serve immediately.

Storage: Store leftovers in an airtight container in the refrigerator for up to 5 days.

Substitute: If you want to add more protein to this pasta dish, try swapping in tempeh strips for the eggplant. You can also use portobello mushrooms to mimic the flavor and texture of meat.

PER SERVING: Calories: 509; Total fat: 20g; Carbohydrates: 60g; Fiber: 7g; Protein: 23g; Calcium: 281mg; Vitamin D: 46mcg; Vitamin B_{12} : 1µg; Iron: 4mg; Zinc: 3mg

Spaghetti and Lentil Balls

MAKES 2 SERVINGS • PREP TIME: 10 MINUTES • COOK TIME: 20 MINUTES

Ingredients

- Kosher salt
- 4 ounces whole wheat spaghetti
- 1 cup cooked lentils
- 1 (15-ounce) can white beans, drained and rinsed
- ¼ cup bread crumbs
- ¼ cup grated Parmesan cheese or nutritional yeast
- ¼ cup chopped fresh parsley
- 1 large egg, beaten
- ½ teaspoon garlic powder
- Kosher salt
- Freshly ground black pepper
- Grapeseed oil or nonstick cooking spray
- 3 cups Rosemary and Thyme Red Sauce or store-bought sauce

Directions:

Step 1.

Fill an 8-quart stockpot three-fourths full of water and add a dash of salt. Bring the water to a boil over high heat and cook the spaghetti according to the package instructions until al dente, about 15 minutes. Drain.

Step 2.

While the pasta is cooking, in a large bowl, mash the lentils and beans with a potato masher or a fork.

Step 3.

Add the bread crumbs, cheese, parsley, egg, garlic powder, and salt and pepper to taste. Use your hands to form the mixture into balls, using about 2 tablespoons to form each ball.

Step 4.

Heat the oil in a large skillet over medium heat. Arrange the balls in a single layer in the skillet and cook for 5 minutes, flip, and cook for an additional 3 minutes, or until the balls are browned on all sides.

Step 5.

Pour the sauce into the skillet and bring to a simmer.

Step 6.

Divide the spaghetti between 2 bowls, top with the "meatballs," and coat with the sauce.

Serve.

Storage: Store the leftovers in an airtight container in the refrigerator for up to 5 days.

Make it easier: Swap in your favorite jarred pasta sauce if you don't have time to make the homemade version. You can also use a can of crushed tomatoes or tomato sauce. Just taste and season with salt, pepper, and additional garlic powder if needed.

PER SERVING: Calories: 620; Total fat: 22g; Carbohydrates: 28g; Fiber: 10g; Protein: 31g; Calcium: 638mg; Vitamin D: 0mcg; Vitamin B_{12}: 1µg; Iron: 8mg; Zinc: 4mg

Creamy Pumpkin-Sage Alfredo

MAKES 2 SERVINGS • PREP TIME: 5 MINUTES • COOK TIME: 20 MINUTES

Ingredients

- Kosher salt
- 4 ounces fettuccine
- 1 tablespoon grapeseed oil
- 2 cups fresh baby spinach
- ½ cup pumpkin puree
- 2 tablespoons minced fresh sage
- 1 cup plain oat milk
- ½ cup shredded Parmesan cheese
- Freshly ground black pepper

Directions:

Step 1.

Fill an 8-quart stockpot three-fourths full of water and add a dash of salt. Bring the water to a boil over high heat and cook the fettuccine according to the package instructions or until al dente, about 15 minutes. Reserve 1 cup of the cooking liquid, then drain the pasta and transfer it to a large bowl.

Step 2.

Rinse the stockpot, then add the oil and heat it over medium heat.

Step 3.

Add the spinach, pumpkin, sage, and milk to the pot and bring to a simmer.

Step 4.

Turn off the heat and add the cheese, stirring to combine.

Step 5.

Add the pasta to the sauce and toss until it is evenly coated. If the sauce is too thick, add a tablespoon of the reserved cooking liquid and toss it again.

Step 6.

Taste and season with salt and pepper. Serve.

Storage: Store the leftover pasta in an airtight container in the refrigerator for up to 5 days.

Mix it up: Instead of spinach, try this pumpkin Alfredo sauce with kale, broccoli, or cauliflower. You can also use basil or parsley instead of sage to give it a new feel.

PER SERVING: Calories: 454; Total fat: 16g; Carbohydrates: 58g; Fiber: 4g; Protein: 20g; Calcium: 423mg; Vitamin D: 1mcg; Vitamin B_{12} : 1µg; Iron: 4mg; Zinc: 3mg

Greek Lasagna

MAKES 8 SERVINGS • PREP TIME: 5 MINUTES • COOK TIME: 1 HOUR

Ingredients

- Grapeseed oil or nonstick cooking spray
- Kosher salt
- 12 ounces whole wheat penne
- 1 (28-ounce) can crushed tomatoes
- 1 tablespoon dried oregano
- 2 cups chopped fresh baby spinach
- 2 (8-ounce) blocks tempeh, crumbled
- 1 cup whole milk
- 1½ cups grated Parmesan cheese
- ½ teaspoon ground nutmeg (optional)
- ⅔ cup plain Greek yogurt
- Chopped fresh parsley (optional)

Directions:

Step 1.

Preheat the oven to 350°F. Grease a 9-by-12-inch baking dish.

Step 2.

Fill a 12-quart stockpot three-fourths full of water and add a dash of salt. Bring the water to a boil over high heat and cook the penne according to the package instructions or until al dente, about 10 minutes. Drain the pasta.

Step 3.

Add the tomatoes, oregano, spinach, and tempeh and transfer the mixture to the baking dish. Add the pasta and stir well.

Step 4.

In a large saucepan, heat the milk, cheese, and nutmeg (if using) over medium heat until simmering, then reduce the heat to medium-low and simmer until the cheese is melted, about

10 minutes.

Step 5.

Remove the sauce from the heat, allow it to cool for a couple of minutes, and then add the Greek yogurt.

Step 6.

Pour the sauce over the pasta mixture in the baking dish and bake for 45 minutes, or until hot and bubbly.

Step 7.

Garnish the dish with fresh parsley (if using) and allow it to cool slightly before cutting it into pieces and serving.

Storage: Store leftover pasta in an airtight container in the refrigerator for up to 5 days.

Protein swaps: If you can't find tempeh, try using lentils or dried peas instead. Opt for precooked packages or prep them ahead of time to make it easier to cook this dish later on.

PER SERVING: Calories: 387; Total fat: 14g; Carbohydrates: 46g; Fiber: 6g; Protein: 24g; Calcium: 347mg; Vitamin D: 0mcg; Vitamin B_{12} : 1µg; Iron: 4mg; Zinc: 3mg

White Bean and Tomato Stuffed Shells

MAKES 8 SERVINGS • PREP TIME: 5 MINUTES • COOK TIME: 30 MINUTES

Ingredients

- Grapeseed oil or nonstick cooking spray
- Kosher salt
- 8 ounces jumbo pasta shells
- 1 (8-ounce) package frozen spinach, thawed
- 2 cups ricotta or Almond Ricotta (twice the recipe)
- 2 (15-ounce) cans cannellini beans, drained and rinsed
- ¼ cup chopped fresh parsley
- 1 large egg, beaten
- 1 (28-ounce) can crushed tomatoes
- 1 tablespoon dried or finely chopped fresh basil
- 1½ cups shredded mozzarella cheese
- ½ cup grated Parmesan or Pecorino Romano cheese

Directions:

Step 1.

Preheat the oven to 350°F. Grease a 9-by-12-inch baking pan.

Step 2.

Place an 8-quart stockpot filled three-fourths full of water and a dash of salt over high heat. Bring to a boil and cook the pasta for half the time on the package instructions, about 5 minutes. Drain.

Step 3.

While the shells are cooking, press the liquid from the spinach and transfer the spinach to a large bowl.

Step 4.

Add the ricotta, beans, parsley, and egg and stir to combine.

Step 5.

Spread one-third of the crushed tomatoes in the baking pan.

Step 6.

Stuff the ricotta mixture into the pasta shells and arrange them in a single layer in the pan.

Step 7.

Pour the remaining tomatoes over the shells and sprinkle with the basil.

Step 8.

Sprinkle the mozzarella and Parmesan cheese on top, and bake the shells for 25 minutes, or until the cheese melts and starts to bubble. Serve immediately.

Storage: Store the leftover pasta in an airtight container in the refrigerator for up to 5 days.

Protein swaps: You can use canned or dried white beans for this recipe. If you use dried beans, cook them ahead. In addition to cannellini, Great Northern beans and chickpeas work well in this recipe.

PER SERVING: Calories: 419; Total fat: 16g; Carbohydrates: 44g; Fiber: 10g; Protein: 26g; Calcium: 415mg; Vitamin D: 0mcg; Vitamin B_{12}: 1µg; Iron: 5mg; Zinc: 3mg

One-Pan Skillet Lasagna

MAKES 2 SERVINGS • PREP TIME: 5 MINUTES • COOK TIME: 25 MINUTES

Ingredients

- 2 tablespoons grapeseed oil
- ¼ cup diced onion
- 1 (8-ounce) block tempeh, crumbled
- 3 garlic cloves, minced
- ⅛ teaspoon kosher salt
- ⅛ teaspoon freshly ground black pepper
- 1 (28-ounce) can crushed tomatoes
- 6 lasagna noodles, broken in half

- ½ cup ricotta or Almond Ricotta
- ½ cup shredded mozzarella cheese

Directions:

Step 1.

Heat the oil in a large skillet (one that has a lid) over medium heat.

Step 2.

Once the oil is shiny, add the onion and cook for 4 minutes, or until translucent.

Step 3.

Add the tempeh, garlic, salt, and pepper and cook for 1 additional minute.

Step 4.

Add the tomatoes and lasagna noodles, then press the noodles down into the tomato sauce. Cover the skillet, and simmer for 15 minutes, or until the noodles are tender. (Add some water if needed to fully cover the noodles as they cook.)

Step 5.

Spoon the ricotta around the noodles in the pan and sprinkle the mozzarella on top.

Step 6.

Cook for 2 minutes more, or until the cheese is melted. Serve immediately.

Storage: Store the leftovers in an airtight container in the refrigerator for up to 5 days.

Substitute: If you can't find tempeh, you can either omit it from the recipe or swap in chopped walnuts. Nuts give this dish some added crunchy texture, and walnuts are also a plant-based source of omega-3s.

PER SERVING: Calories: 260; Total fat: 11g; Carbohydrates: 29g; Fiber: 3g; Protein: 14g; Calcium: 124mg; Vitamin D: 0mcg; Vitamin B_{12}: 0µg; Iron: 4mg; Zinc: 1mg

Spinach Spaghetti Pie

MAKES 6 SERVINGS • PREP TIME: 5 MINUTES • COOK TIME: 25 MINUTES

Ingredients

- Grapeseed oil or nonstick cooking spray
- 1 large egg, lightly beaten
- 2 cups cooked spaghetti 2 cups chopped fresh baby spinach
- 2 tablespoons olive oil
- 1 cup ricotta or Almond Ricotta
- 1 (15-ounce) can crushed tomatoes
- 1 cup shredded mozzarella cheese
- 1 teaspoon dried oregano (optional)
- ½ teaspoon red pepper flakes (optional)

Directions:

Step 1.

Preheat the oven to 350°F. Lightly grease a 10-inch pie dish.

Step 2.

Place the egg, spaghetti, spinach, and olive oil in a large bowl and mix well. Transfer to the pie dish, spreading the mixture out to form a thin layer.

Step 3.

Add spoonfuls of the ricotta on top, then add the tomatoes.

Step 4.

Sprinkle with the mozzarella, oregano (if using), and red pepper flakes (if using).

Step 5.

Bake the dish for 25 minutes, or until the cheese melts and starts to bubble. Serve immediately.

Mix it up: Give this spaghetti pie more of a summery feel with traditional Caprese toppings. Top the spaghetti crust with fresh heirloom tomatoes instead of canned and fresh mozzarella instead of shredded. After it's cooked, garnish the pie with chopped fresh basil.

Storage: Store leftovers in an airtight container in the refrigerator for up to 5 days.

PER SERVING: Calories: 233; Total fat: 15g; Carbohydrates: 14g; Fiber: 3g; Protein: 12g; Calcium: 213mg; Vitamin D: 0mcg; Vitamin B_{12}: 1µg; Iron: 2mg; Zinc: 2mg

Vegan Cannelloni

MAKES 2 SERVINGS • PREP TIME: 15 MINUTES • COOK TIME: 25 MINUTES

Ingredients

- Kosher salt
- 4 ounces cannelloni pasta
- Grapeseed oil or nonstick cooking spray
- 1 (15-ounce) can crushed tomatoes
- 1 (8-ounce) package frozen spinach, thawed
- 1 cup Almond Ricotta or store-bought vegan ricotta
- 1 garlic clove, minced (or use garlic powder)
- ¼ teaspoon freshly ground black pepper
- Chopped fresh basil (optional)

Directions:

Step 1.

Fill a large saucepan three-fourths full of water, add a dash of salt, and bring to a boil over high heat. Add the pasta and cook according to the package instructions. Drain.

Step 2.

Preheat the oven to 350°F. Lightly grease an 8-by-11-inch baking pan.

Step 3.

Spread a layer of crushed tomatoes in the baking pan.

Step 4.

Squeeze out the extra water from the spinach, then transfer the spinach to a large bowl and add the almond ricotta, garlic, ¼ teaspoon salt, and the pepper, stirring to combine.

Step 5.

Cut a corner tip off the bottom of a zippered plastic bag and fill the bag with the spinach-ricotta mixture. Pipe the mixture into the pasta tubes and arrange the tubes in the baking pan.

Step 6.

Spoon the remaining tomatoes over the pasta and bake for 25 minutes, or until warmed through.

Step 7.

Garnish the dish with chopped fresh basil, if desired, and serve.

Storage: Store the leftovers in an airtight container in the refrigerator for up to 5 days.

Tip: Stir a can of white beans into the tomato sauce for extra protein. Just be sure to drain and rinse the beans first.

PER SERVING: Calories: 591; Total fat: 32g; Carbohydrates: 40g; Fiber: 5g; Protein: 35g; Calcium: 609mg; Vitamin D: 1mcg; Vitamin B_{12} : 1µg; Iron: 5mg; Zinc: 4mg

Cheesy Broccoli Pasta Bake

MAKES 8 SERVINGS • PREP TIME: 5 MINUTES • COOK TIME: 40 MINUTES

Ingredients

- 3 tablespoons grapeseed oil, plus more for the baking dish
- Kosher salt
- 12 ounces whole wheat rotini
- ½ medium onion, diced
- 2 (8-ounce) blocks tempeh, crumbled
- 1 teaspoon dried oregano
- 1 teaspoon dried basil
- ¼ teaspoon freshly ground black pepper
- 4 cups chopped broccoli florets
- 1 (28-ounce) can crushed tomatoes
- 1 cup shredded mozzarella cheese

- ½ cup shredded Parmesan cheese (or additional mozzarella)

Directions:

Step 1.

Preheat the oven to 350°F. Lightly grease a 9-by-12-inch baking dish (if you are not using a Dutch oven).

Step 2.

Bring a large saucepan filled three-fourths full of water with a dash of salt to a boil over high heat. Add the pasta and cook for 8 minutes, or according to the package instructions. Drain.

Step 3.

Heat the 3 tablespoons oil in a Dutch oven (or large skillet) over medium heat.

Step 4.

Once the oil is shiny, add the onion and cook for 4 minutes or until translucent.

Step 5.

Add the tempeh, oregano, basil, ¼ teaspoon salt, the pepper, and broccoli and cook for 3 minutes, or until the broccoli is bright green. Turn off the heat.

Step 6.

Add the tomatoes, stirring to combine, then add the pasta, stirring until it is evenly coated with the sauce.

Step 7.

Transfer the mixture to the baking dish (if you're not using a Dutch oven). Sprinkle the mixture with the mozzarella and Parmesan.

Step 8.

Bake the casserole for 25 minutes, or until the cheese is melted and bubbling. Move the dish to the broiler during the final couple of minutes, if desired (do not move a Dutch oven to the broiler). Allow to cool for 5 minutes, then serve.

Storage: Store the leftovers in an airtight container in the refrigerator for up to 5 days.

Protein swap: Omit the tempeh, if desired. You can also swap in white beans or cooked lentils for another source of plant-based protein.

PER SERVING: Calories: 427; Total fat: 17g; Carbohydrates: 51g; Fiber: 7g; Protein: 25g; Calcium: 249mg; Vitamin D: 0mcg; Vitamin B_{12} : 0μg; Iron: 5mg; Zinc: 3mg

Watermelon Poke Bowls

MAKES 2 SERVINGS • PREP TIME: 10 MINUTES, PLUS 30 MINUTES TO MARINATE

Ingredients

- 2 tablespoons soy sauce
- 1 tablespoon toasted sesame oil
- 2 teaspoons rice vinegar
- ¼ teaspoon ground ginger
- 2 cups cubed seedless watermelon
- 1 scallion, both white and green parts, chopped
- 1 cup cooked brown rice (see Tip)
- 1 cup steamed shelled edamame
- 1 nori sheet, torn into pieces
- 1 avocado, peeled, pitted, and sliced

Directions:

Step 1.
In a medium bowl, whisk the soy sauce, sesame oil, vinegar, and ginger until well combined.

Step 2.
Add the watermelon and scallion and marinate for at least 30 minutes or cover and chill in the refrigerator overnight.

Step 3.
Divide the rice into 2 bowls and add the edamame, nori, and avocado.

Step 4.
Top with the marinated watermelon.

Step 5.
Drizzle the remaining marinade over the bowls, if desired. Serve.

Storage: Store leftovers in an airtight container in the refrigerator for up to 2 days.

Protein swaps: Instead of the steamed edamame in these bowls, try swapping in crispy tofu, which has been sautéed in a lightly greased skillet for 4 minutes on each side, or until golden and crisp.

PER SERVING: Calories: 505; Total fat: 27g; Carbohydrates: 56g; Fiber: 15g; Protein: 16g; Calcium: 96mg; Vitamin D: 0mcg; Vitamin B_{12} : 0µg; Iron: 3mg; Zinc: 3mg

Moroccan-Inspired Chickpea Couscous

MAKES 2 SERVINGS • PREP TIME: 5 MINUTES • COOK TIME: 20 MINUTES

Ingredients

- 1½ cups water
- 1 cup traditional couscous
- 1 tablespoon grapeseed oil
- ¼ cup diced onion

- 1 teaspoon ground cumin
- ½ teaspoon ground turmeric
- ¼ teaspoon kosher salt
- ¼ teaspoon freshly ground black pepper
- 2 teaspoons olive oil
- 1 (15-ounce) can chickpeas, drained and rinsed
- 2 tablespoons chopped fresh cilantro
- 2 tablespoons chopped fresh mint
- ¼ cup slivered almonds
- ¼ cup raisins

Directions:

Step 1.

In a medium saucepan, bring the water to a boil over high heat, remove it from the heat, stir in the couscous, cover, and let stand for 10 minutes. Fluff with a fork and set aside.

Step 2.

Heat the grapeseed oil in a large skillet (that has a lid) over medium heat.

Step 3.

Once the oil is shiny, add the onion and cook for 4 minutes or until the onion is translucent.

Step 4.

Add the cumin, turmeric, salt, and pepper and cook for 1 minute or until aromatic.

Step 5.

Turn off the heat and add the olive oil, the couscous, the chickpeas, cilantro, mint, almonds, and raisins.

Step 6.

Taste and adjust the seasoning, if needed. Serve.

Storage: Store any leftovers in an airtight container in the refrigerator for up to 1 week.

Substitute: Many different kinds of dried fruits would be delicious in this recipe. Instead of raisins, try dried cherries, currants, apricots, or dates. If you want to try fresh fruit, use halved grapes or pitted cherries.

PER SERVING: Calories: 723; Total fat: 22g; Carbohydrates: 108g; Fiber: 16g; Protein: 25g; Calcium: 133mg; Vitamin D: 0mcg; Vitamin B_{12} : 0µg; Iron: 6mg; Zinc: 3mg

Pinto Bean Tostadas with Red Cabbage and Cilantro Slaw

MAKES 2 SERVINGS • PREP TIME: 5 MINUTES • COOK TIME: 10 MINUTES

Ingredients

- 4 (4-inch) corn tortillas
- 1 teaspoon grapeseed oil
- Kosher salt
- 1 (15-ounce) can pinto beans, drained and rinsed
- ¼ cup vegetable broth or water
- 1 teaspoon ground cumin
- 1 teaspoon chili powder
- ½ teaspoon garlic powder
- ⅛ teaspoon cayenne (optional)
- 1 cup Red Cabbage and Cilantro Slaw

Directions:

Step 1.
Preheat the oven or toaster oven to 400°F. Line a baking sheet with parchment.

Step 2.
Brush the tortillas with the oil, sprinkle with salt, and spread on the baking sheet in a single layer.

Step 3.
Bake the tortillas for 8 minutes, flipping halfway through, or until crispy. Cool the tortillas on a rack for 15 minutes.

Step 4.
While the tortillas are baking, in a large saucepan, stir together the pinto beans, broth or water, cumin, chili powder, and garlic powder over medium heat.

Step 5.
Cook for 5 minutes, or until warmed through and the broth is absorbed.

Step 6.
Taste and season with salt, if needed.

Step 7.
Mash the bean mixture with a potato masher or a fork and divide it evenly among the tortillas, spreading it out.

Step 8.
Spoon the Red Cabbage and Cilantro Slaw on top. Serve immediately.

Make it easier: Crispy tostada shells are often available at the supermarket; look for them near the tortillas. You can also use a premixed vegetable slaw instead of the prepared slaw.

PER SERVING: Calories: 324; Total fat: 5g; Carbohydrates: 58g; Fiber: 15g; Protein: 15g; Calcium: 165mg; Vitamin D: 0mcg; Vitamin B_{12} : 0µg; Iron: 5mg; Zinc: 2mg

Vegan Garlic-Mushroom Naan Pizzas

MAKES 2 SERVINGS • PREP TIME: 5 MINUTES • COOK TIME: 15 MINUTES

Ingredients

- 1 tablespoon grapeseed oil, plus more as needed
- ½ cup sliced fresh mushrooms
- 4 garlic cloves, sliced
- 1 teaspoon balsamic vinegar
- 2 tablespoons nutritional yeast
- ¼ teaspoon kosher salt
- ⅛ teaspoon freshly ground black pepper
- 2 vegan naan flatbreads
- ½ cup tomato sauce
- 1 teaspoon dried oregano
- ½ teaspoon red pepper flakes (optional)

Directions:

Step 1.

Preheat the oven or toaster oven to 400°F. Grease a baking sheet or line it with parchment.

Step 2.

Heat the 1 tablespoon oil in a large skillet over medium heat.

Step 3.

Add the mushrooms and garlic and cook for 4 minutes or until the mushrooms are tender and darker in color.

Step 4.

Turn off the heat and add the vinegar, nutritional yeast, salt, and pepper, stirring to combine.

Step 5.

Lay the naan on the baking sheet and spread half the tomato sauce on each bread, leaving about ½ inch space around the edge.

Step 6.

Divide the mushroom mixture between the breads.

Step 7.

Sprinkle the pizzas with the oregano and red pepper flakes (if using) and bake for 10 minutes, or until the crusts are golden. Serve immediately.

Substitute: Nutritional yeast is a delicious vegan alternative to cheese. Look for it in the bulk section or natural foods aisle. If you can't find nutritional yeast, try subbing with a nut-based cheese, such as the Almond Ricotta . You can also top the breads with fresh or shredded mozzarella, if you include dairy foods.

PER SERVING: Calories: 386; Total fat: 12g; Carbohydrates: 56g; Fiber: 5g; Protein: 15g; Calcium: 117mg; Vitamin D: 0mcg; Vitamin B$_{12}$: 0µg; Iron: 5mg; Zinc: 2mg

Easy Edamame Stir-Fry

MAKES 2 SERVINGS • PREP TIME: 10 MINUTES • COOK TIME: 10 MINUTES

Ingredients

- 2 tablespoons soy sauce
- 1 tablespoon rice vinegar
- 1 tablespoon toasted sesame oil
- 1 teaspoon ground ginger
- 1 teaspoon maple syrup
- ½ teaspoon garlic powder
- 2 tablespoons grapeseed oil
- 4 cups chopped broccoli florets
- 1 cup frozen shelled edamame

OPTIONAL TOPPINGS

- 1 scallion, both white and green parts, chopped
- 1 tablespoon sesame seeds

Directions:

Step 1.

In a small bowl, whisk together the soy sauce, vinegar, sesame oil, ginger, maple syrup, and garlic powder.

Step 2.

Heat the grapeseed oil in a large skillet or wok over medium-high heat.

Step 3.

Add the broccoli and cook for 3 minutes or until bright green.

Step 4.

Add the edamame and the soy sauce mixture and cook until warmed through.

Step 5.

Garnish the dish with the scallions and sesame seeds, if desired.

Mix it up: The nice thing about a stir-fry is that you can use pretty much any vegetable you have in your kitchen. I often make this recipe with whatever fresh produce I need to use up before it goes bad. Try bok choy, cauliflower, carrots, or bell peppers.

PER SERVING: Calories: 361; Total fat: 25g; Carbohydrates: 24g; Fiber: 9g; Protein: 15g; Calcium: 145mg; Vitamin D: 0mcg; Vitamin B$_{12}$: 0µg; Iron: 4mg; Zinc: 2mg

Roasted Chickpea and Carrot Dinner

MAKES 2 SERVINGS • PREP TIME: 10 MINUTES • COOK TIME: 30 MINUTES

Ingredients

- 2 tablespoons grapeseed oil, plus more for greasing the baking sheet
- 1 tablespoon apple cider vinegar
- 1 teaspoon ground cumin
- ½ teaspoon onion powder
- ½ teaspoon garlic powder
- ¼ teaspoon kosher salt
- ¼ teaspoon freshly ground black pepper
- 1 (15-ounce) can chickpeas, drained and rinsed
- 1 pound fresh carrots, halved (5 medium)

OPTIONAL FOR SERVING

- ½ cup chopped fresh cilantro
- ¾ cup Lemon Tahini Dressing or store-bought sauce
- Cooked brown rice

Directions:

Step 1.

Preheat the oven to 450°F. Grease or line a rimmed baking sheet with parchment.

Step 2.

In a large bowl, whisk together the 2 tablespoons oil, the vinegar, cumin, onion powder, garlic powder, salt, and pepper until well blended.

Step 3.

Dry the chickpeas with a clean towel and add them along with the carrots to the bowl with the dressing, and stir until evenly coated.

Step 4.

Spread the mixture on the baking sheet and bake for 30 minutes or until the carrots are tender and the chickpeas are golden and crispy.

Step 5.

Divide the mixture between 2 bowls and serve with the cilantro, tahini dressing and brown rice, if desired.

Storage: Store any leftovers in an airtight container in the refrigerator for up to 1 week. Reheat in the oven for best results.

Mix it up: My favorite way to serve this dish is to drizzle it with the creamy and tangy tahini dressing but you can also try it with a vinaigrette or salsa and guacamole for a Mexican-inspired twist. Instead of brown rice, serve the dish over cooked farro, quinoa, or barley.

PER SERVING: Calories: 425; Total fat: 18g; Carbohydrates: 57g; Fiber: 16g; Protein: 13g; Calcium: 149mg; Vitamin D: 0mcg; Vitamin B_{12} : 0µg; Iron: 5mg; Zinc: 3mg

Sesame Tofu and Broccoli

MAKES 2 SERVINGS • PREP TIME: 10 MINUTES • COOK TIME: 15 MINUTES

Ingredients

- 1 tablespoon grapeseed oil
- ½ (14-ounce) block extra-firm tofu, drained, pressed (see Tip), and cubed
- 4 cups chopped broccoli florets
- 1 (1-inch) piece of fresh ginger, peeled and grated
- 2 garlic cloves, sliced
- ¼ cup vegetable broth
- 2 tablespoons soy sauce
- 1 tablespoon rice vinegar
- 1 tablespoon toasted sesame oil
- 1 teaspoon maple syrup
- 1 tablespoon sesame seeds, toasted if desired

Directions:

Step 1.
Heat the grapeseed oil in a large skillet or wok over medium heat.

Step 2.
Add the tofu and cook for 4 minutes each side, or until golden. Transfer to a plate.

Step 3.
Add the broccoli, ginger, garlic, and broth to the skillet and cook for 5 minutes or until the broccoli is tender.

Step 4.
In a small bowl, whisk together the soy sauce, vinegar, sesame oil, maple syrup, and sesame seeds until well blended.

Step 5.
Pour the sauce into the skillet. Add the cooked tofu, toss, and serve warm.

Storage: Store the leftovers in an airtight container in the refrigerator for up to 1 week.

Protein swaps: Shelled edamame, which is another soy-based food like tofu, makes an ideal substitute in Asian-inspired dishes like this one. For a soy-free alternative, try making this dish with scrambled eggs instead. Scramble the eggs, transfer them to a plate, and cook the rest of the recipe as usual, stirring the cooked eggs back in just before serving.

PER SERVING: Calories: 321; Total fat: 22g; Carbohydrates: 20g; Fiber: 6g; Protein: 17g; Calcium: 279mg; Vitamin D: 0mcg; Vitamin B_{12} : 0µg; Iron: 4mg; Zinc: 2mg

Black Bean Burrito Bowl

MAKES 2 SERVINGS • PREP TIME: 5 MINUTES • COOK TIME: 6 MINUTES

Ingredients

- 1 tablespoon grapeseed oil
- ¼ cup diced red onion
- 1 (15-ounce) can black beans, drained and rinsed
- 1 cup frozen or canned corn kernels
- 1 cup chopped fresh kale or fresh baby spinach
- 1 tablespoon fresh lime juice
- 2 teaspoons ground cumin
- 1 teaspoon chili powder
- ¼ teaspoon kosher salt
- ⅛ teaspoon freshly ground black pepper

OPTIONAL FOR SERVING
- Cooked brown rice
- Fresh cilantro
- Sliced avocado

Directions:

Step 1.
Heat the oil in a large skillet over medium heat.

Step 2.
Once the oil is shiny, add the onion and cook for 3 minutes, or until translucent.

Step 3.
Add the black beans, corn, kale, lime juice, cumin, chili powder, salt, and pepper and cook for 3 minutes, or until warmed through and the kale is wilted.

Step 4.
Serve with brown rice, cilantro, and avocado, if desired.

Storage: Store leftovers in an airtight container and refrigerate for up to 1 week. Wait to slice the avocado until immediately before serving.

Protein swaps: Canned black beans are a convenient staple for adding protein to Mexican-inspired dishes. Dried beans also work great, and you can swap in pinto or red kidney varieties to change the flavor. For another twist, try lentils or scrambled eggs.

PER SERVING: Calories: 353; Total fat: 9g; Carbohydrates: 57g; Fiber: 17g; Protein: 17g; Calcium: 167mg; Vitamin D: 0mcg; Vitamin B$_{12}$: 0μg; Iron: 6mg; Zinc: 3mg

Apple Chips with Cinnamon-Yogurt Dip

MAKES 2 SERVINGS • PREP TIME: 5 MINUTES • COOK TIME: 50 MINUTES

Ingredients

- 1 apple, cored and sliced ⅛ inch thick
- 1 cup plain Greek yogurt
- 2 teaspoons maple syrup
- ½ teaspoon ground cinnamon
- ½ teaspoon vanilla extract (optional)
- ⅛ teaspoon kosher salt
- 2 tablespoons chopped nuts (optional)

Directions:

Step 1.
Preheat the oven or toaster oven to 275°F. Line a baking sheet with parchment or baking mat.

Step 2.
Spread the apple slices in a single layer on the baking sheet and bake for 50 minutes, or until golden and crispy. Cool the chips on a rack. The apples will continue to get crispy as they cool.

Step 3.
While the chips are baking, in a small bowl, stir together the yogurt, maple syrup, cinnamon, vanilla (if using), and salt until blended.

Step 4.
Top the dip with chopped nuts (if using) and serve with the baked apple chips.

Storage: Store the dip in an airtight container in the refrigerator for up to 1 week. Store the apple chips in an airtight container at room temperature for up to 6 months.

Substitute: For a vegan alternative to this Greek yogurt dip, substitute a plain dairy-free yogurt alternative. You can find vegan yogurts made from coconut, soy, almond, or oat milk in the dairy section of most grocery stores.

PER SERVING: Calories: 141; Total fat: 5g; Carbohydrates: 23g; Fiber: 3g; Protein: 5g; Calcium: 167mg; Vitamin D: 0mcg; Vitamin B$_{12}$: 0μg; Iron: 0mg; Zinc: 1mg

Fruit and Nut Energy Bites

MAKES 8 SERVINGS • PREP TIME: 10 MINUTES

Ingredients

- 1¼ cups pitted dates, chopped
- ¾ cup walnut halves and pieces
- ½ cup blanched almonds
- 2 tablespoons ground flaxseed
- 1 teaspoon ground cinnamon
- 1 teaspoon vanilla extract
- ¼ teaspoon kosher salt

Directions:

Step 1.

Place the dates, walnuts, almonds, flaxseed, cinnamon, vanilla, and salt in a food processor and pulse until a sticky dough forms. It should stick together when pressed between your fingers.

Step 2.

Take about 2 tablespoons of the dough and use your hands to roll it into a ball. Repeat with the remaining dough. Enjoy.

Storage: Store the balls in an airtight container in the refrigerator for up to 2 weeks or freeze for up to 3 months.

Protein swaps: You can use any combination of nuts to make these plant-based energy bites. For a nut-free alternative, try a mix of pumpkin and sunflower seeds.

PER SERVING: Calories: 200; Total fat: 12g; Carbohydrates: 22g; Fiber: 4g; Protein: 4g; Calcium: 52mg; Vitamin D: 0mcg; Vitamin B_{12} : 0μg; Iron: 1mg; Zinc: 1mg

No-Bake Chocolate–Peanut Butter Bars

MAKES 4 SERVINGS • PREP TIME: 10 MINUTES

Ingredients

- 1½ cups chopped pitted dates
- 1 cup walnut halves and pieces
- ¼ cup peanut butter
- 2 tablespoons unsweetened cocoa powder
- 2 teaspoons vanilla extract

Directions:

Step 1.

Place the dates, walnuts, peanut butter, cocoa powder, and vanilla in food processor and pulse until a sticky dough forms. It should stick together when pressed between your fingers.

Step 2.

Line a loaf pan with parchment paper and press the dough into the pan evenly.

Step 3.

Chill the mixture in the refrigerator for at least 1 hour.

Step 4.

Remove the chilled dough from the pan by lifting it out using the parchment paper and transfer to a cutting board. Cut into 4 bars.

Storage: Store the bars in an airtight container in the refrigerator for up to 2 weeks or freeze for up to 3 months.

Substitute: If you're looking for an alternative to peanuts, try making these energy bars with sunflower seed butter or tahini. Instead of walnuts, try almonds, pecans, or cashews.

PER SERVING: Calories: 455; Total fat: 27g; Carbohydrates: 51g; Fiber: 8g; Protein: 10g; Calcium: 61mg; Vitamin D: 0mcg; Vitamin B_{12} : 0µg; Iron: 2mg; Zinc: 2mg

Sesame-Ginger Edamame

MAKES 2 SERVINGS • PREP TIME: 2 MINUTES • COOK TIME: 5 MINUTES

Ingredients

- Grapeseed oil or nonstick cooking spray
- 2¼ cups frozen edamame, in pods
- 1-inch piece of ginger, peeled and grated
- 1 tablespoon toasted sesame oil
- 1 teaspoon rice vinegar
- 1 teaspoon soy sauce
- 1 teaspoon maple syrup
- Kosher salt

Directions:

Step 1.

Lightly oil a large skillet or wok and heat it over medium heat.

Step 2.

Add the frozen edamame and cook until thawed.

Step 3.

Add the ginger, sesame oil, vinegar, soy sauce, and maple syrup and cook for 3 minutes, or until warmed through.

Step 4.

Season the mixture with salt and serve.

Storage: Store the leftovers in an airtight container in the refrigerator for up to 1 week.

Mix it up: Switch up the spices when you're making edamame for snacking. Try garlic powder or cayenne pepper for a spicy twist.

PER SERVING: Calories: 286; Total fat: 16g; Carbohydrates: 20g; Fiber: 9g; Protein: 19g; Calcium: 114mg; Vitamin D: 0mcg; Vitamin B_{12} : 0µg; Iron: 4mg; Zinc: 2mg

Cheesy Vegan Popcorn

MAKES 2 SERVINGS • PREP TIME: 2 MINUTES • COOK TIME: 5 MINUTES

Ingredients

- 1 tablespoon coconut oil
- ¼ cup popcorn kernels
- 2 tablespoons nutritional yeast
- ½ teaspoon garlic powder
- ½ teaspoon onion powder
- ¼ teaspoon kosher salt
- ⅛ teaspoon freshly ground black pepper

Directions:

Step 1.

Heat the coconut oil in a 12-quart stockpot over medium heat.

Step 2.

When the oil is melted, pour in the popcorn kernels and cover the pot.

Step 3.

Cook for 5 minutes, shaking the pot occasionally to promote even cooking, or until all of the popcorn kernels are popped.

Step 4.

Add the nutritional yeast, garlic powder, onion powder, salt, and pepper and shake the pot to mix. Serve.

Storage: Store the popcorn in an airtight container for up to 1 day.

Mix it up: Popcorn is a healthy snack that tastes good all on its own or with just a sprinkle of salt. For a change, try using Cajun seasoning, curry powder, or a little hot sauce.

PER SERVING: Calories: 165; Total fat: 8g; Carbohydrates: 18g; Fiber: 4g; Protein: 2g;

Calcium: 15mg; Vitamin D: 0mcg; Vitamin B$_{12}$: 0µg; Iron: 1mg; Zinc: 0mg

Chili-Lime Tortilla Chips

MAKES 4 SERVINGS • PREP TIME: 5 MINUTES • COOK TIME: 10 MINUTES

Ingredients

- 8 (4-inch) corn tortillas
- ¼ cup grapeseed oil
- 2 tablespoons fresh lime juice (from 1 medium)
- 1 teaspoon chili powder
- Kosher salt

Directions:

Step 1.

Preheat the oven or toaster oven to 400°F. Line 2 baking sheets with parchment.

Step 2.

Cut the tortillas into triangles and spread them in a single layer on the baking sheets.

Step 3.

In a small bowl, whisk together the oil, lime juice, and chili powder and brush the mixture on each side of the tortilla chips.

Step 4.

Sprinkle the tortilla chips with salt and transfer the baking sheets to the oven. Bake for 10 minutes, flipping halfway through, or until the chips are golden and crispy.

Step 5.

Cool the chips on a rack before serving. The chips will continue to get crispier as they cool.

Storage: Store the chips in an airtight container for up to 1 week.

Make it easier: Want to make this homemade snack super simple and easy? Leave out the lime juice and chili powder, and you'll still get a great-tasting crunchy corn chip that's perfect for dipping into salsa or guacamole.

PER SERVING: Calories: 177; Total fat: 14g; Carbohydrates: 12g; Fiber: 2g; Protein: 1g; Calcium: 23mg; Vitamin D: 0mcg; Vitamin B$_{12}$: 0µg; Iron: 0mg; Zinc: 0mg

Roasted Potatoes with Lemon-Chive Yogurt Dip

MAKES 4 SERVINGS • PREP TIME: 5 MINUTES • COOK TIME: 25 MINUTES

Ingredients

- 4 medium russet or Yukon Gold potatoes, cut into 1-inch cubes

- 2 tablespoons grapeseed oil
- ½ teaspoon onion powder
- ½ teaspoon garlic powder
- ¼ teaspoon kosher salt
- ¼ teaspoon freshly ground black pepper
- 1 cup plain Greek yogurt
- 2 tablespoons chopped fresh chives
- 1 tablespoon fresh lemon juice
- ¼ teaspoon maple syrup

Directions:

Step 1.

Preheat the oven to 450°F. Line a baking sheet with parchment.

Step 2.

In a large bowl, toss together the potatoes, oil, onion powder, garlic powder, salt, and pepper, and spread out in a single layer on the baking sheet.

Step 3.

Bake the potatoes for 25 minutes, stirring halfway through, or until golden and crispy. Set aside until cooled enough to handle, about 15 minutes.

Step 4.

While the potatoes are baking, in a small bowl, stir together the yogurt, chives, lemon juice, and maple syrup until blended. Season the dip with salt and pepper.

Step 5.

Serve the dip with the roasted potatoes.

Storage: Store the leftovers in an airtight container in the refrigerator for up to 5 days.

Substitute: This recipe will work with any type of chopped root vegetable, including Yukon Gold potatoes, Red Bliss potatoes, parsnips, carrots, or sweet potatoes.

PER SERVING: Calories: 266; Total fat: 9g; Carbohydrates: 41g; Fiber: 5g; Protein: 7g; Calcium: 103mg; Vitamin D: 0mcg; Vitamin B_{12}: 0µg; Iron: 2mg; Zinc: 1mg

Vegetable Spring Rolls

MAKES 6 SERVINGS • PREP TIME: 20 MINUTES

Ingredients

- 6 spring roll wrappers
- 1 cup thinly sliced cucumber
- 1 cup shredded carrots
- ½ cup fresh cilantro

- ¼ cup Sesame Ginger Dressing or store-bought sauce

Directions:

Step 1.

Dip a wrap in water until it's flexible and lay it on a flat surface.

Step 2.

Arrange one-sixth of the cucumber, carrots, and cilantro in the center of the rice paper.

Step 3.

Fold up the side edges and roll up the wrapper from the far end to form a sealed roll.

Step 4.

Repeat with the remaining wrappers, using all of the vegetable mix.

Step 5.

Serve the rolls with the sauce for dipping.

Mix it up: Cabbage, bell peppers, fresh basil, scallions, and pickled vegetables all make delicious additions to the spring rolls. Use whatever you have in your refrigerator to help reduce food waste.

Storage: Store the leftovers in an airtight container in the refrigerator for up to 2 days.

PER SERVING: Calories: 120; Total fat: 6g; Carbohydrates: 13g; Fiber: 1g; Protein: 2g; Calcium: 13mg; Vitamin D: 0mcg; Vitamin B_{12} : 0μg; Iron: 0mg; Zinc: 0mg

Tofu Nuggets

MAKES 2 SERVINGS • PREP TIME: 5 MINUTES • COOK TIME: 40 MINUTES

Ingredients

- ¼ cup whole wheat flour (or other flour of choice)
- 2 tablespoons cornstarch
- ½ teaspoon onion powder
- ½ teaspoon garlic powder
- ½ teaspoon kosher salt
- ½ (14-ounce) block extra-firm tofu, drained and pressed (see Tip)
- 2 tablespoons grapeseed oil

Directions:

Step 1.

Preheat the oven to 450°F. Line a baking sheet with parchment or a silicone baking mat.

Step 2.

In a large bowl, stir together the flour, cornstarch, onion powder, garlic powder, and salt until blended.

Step 3.

Tear the tofu into bite-size pieces and add to the bowl.

Step 4.

Add the oil to the bowl and use your hands to toss the tofu until it's evenly coated.

Step 5.

Dust off the extra flour and spread the tofu on the baking sheet.

Step 6.

Bake the tofu for 40 minutes, or until golden and crispy.

Step 7.

Cool the tofu on a rack before serving.

Storage: Store the leftovers in an airtight container in the refrigerator for up to 1 week.

Mix it up: Tofu is a blank slate when it comes to flavor, so you have lots of opportunities to add spices to the breading to take things up a notch. Try dried basil, Jamaican jerk seasoning, or nutritional yeast for a cheesy flavor.

PER SERVING: Calories: 310; Total fat: 20g; Carbohydrates: 21g; Fiber: 2g; Protein: 13g; Calcium: 208mg; Vitamin D: 0mcg; Vitamin B_{12} : 0μg; Iron: 3mg; Zinc: 2mg

Buffalo Cauliflower

MAKES 4 SERVINGS • PREP TIME: 5 MINUTES • COOK TIME: 40 MINUTES

Ingredients

- ¼ cup whole wheat flour (or other flour of choice)
- 2 tablespoons cornstarch
- ½ teaspoon onion powder
- ½ teaspoon garlic powder
- ½ teaspoon kosher salt
- 1 medium head of cauliflower, cut into large florets
- ¼ cup grapeseed oil
- ¼ cup buffalo-style hot sauce
- 1 scallion, both white and green parts, chopped (optional)

Directions:

Step 1.

Preheat the oven to 450°F. Line a baking sheet with parchment or a silicone baking mat.

Step 2.

In a large bowl, stir together the flour, cornstarch, onion powder, garlic powder, and salt until well mixed. Add the cauliflower and toss to combine.

Step 3.
Add the oil to the bowl and use your hands to toss the cauliflower until it's evenly coated.

Step 4.
Spread the cauliflower in a single layer on the baking sheet.

Step 5.
Roast the cauliflower for 40 minutes, or until golden and crispy.

Step 6.
While the cauliflower is baking, pour the hot sauce into a large bowl.

Step 7.
Cool the cauliflower on a rack for 5 minutes.

Step 8.
Add the cooked cauliflower to the sauce and toss until it is evenly coated with sauce.

Step 9.
Garnish with the scallion, if desired, and serve immediately.

Storage: Store any leftovers in an airtight container in the refrigerator for up to 1 week.

Make it easier: If you don't care a lot about getting crunchy texture, you can easily make this recipe without the flour, cornstarch, and onion and garlic powders. The cauliflower will still get golden and roasted without the breading, and it'll have plenty of flavor from the hot sauce.

PER SERVING: Calories: 202; Total fat: 14g; Carbohydrates: 17g; Fiber: 4g; Protein: 4g; Calcium: 38mg; Vitamin D: 0mcg; Vitamin B_{12} : 0μg; Iron: 1mg; Zinc: 1mg

Garlicky Roasted Chickpeas

MAKES 2 SERVINGS • PREP TIME: 5 MINUTES • COOK TIME: 20 MINUTES

Ingredients

- 1 (15-ounce) can chickpeas, drained and rinsed
- 2 tablespoons grapeseed oil
- 1 teaspoon garlic powder
- ½ teaspoon onion powder
- ¼ teaspoon kosher salt
- ¼ teaspoon freshly ground black pepper

Directions:

Step 1.
Preheat the oven or toaster oven to 400°F. Line a baking sheet with parchment.

Step 2.

Use paper towels to dry the chickpeas and then transfer them to a large bowl.

Step 3.

Add the oil, garlic powder, onion powder, salt, and pepper to the bowl and toss to combine.

Step 4.

Spread the chickpeas in a single layer on the baking sheet and bake for 20 minutes, or until golden and crispy. Serve.

Storage: Store the chickpeas in an airtight container for up to 1 week.

Mix it up: Try roasted chickpeas with any of your favorite seasoning blends. Try taco seasoning, curry powder, Cajun seasoning, or a Jamaican jerk spice blend.

PER SERVING: Calories: 329; Total fat: 17g; Carbohydrates: 35g; Fiber: 10g; Protein: 11g; Calcium: 64mg; Vitamin D: 0mcg; Vitamin B_{12} : 0µg; Iron: 4mg; Zinc: 2mg

Black Bean Quesadillas

MAKES 2 SERVINGS • PREP TIME: 5 MINUTES • COOK TIME: 10 MINUTES

Ingredients

- 1 cup cooked black beans
- 1 cup chopped fresh baby spinach
- ½ cup chopped fresh cilantro
- 1 jalapeño pepper, sliced
- ¼ teaspoon kosher salt
- Grapeseed oil or nonstick cooking spray
- 4 (10-inch) flour tortillas
- 1 cup shredded pepper jack cheese

Directions:

Step 1.

In a medium bowl, combine the beans, spinach, cilantro, jalapeño, and salt.

Step 2.

Lightly oil a large skillet and preheat it on medium heat.

Step 3.

Place 1 tortilla in the skillet and spread one-fourth of the bean filling on one side of the tortilla. Sprinkle the filling with one-fourth of the cheese, and fold over the tortilla to cover the filling.

Step 4.

Cook for 5 minutes or until the bottom turns golden brown, and then flip the tortilla over and cook for an additional 5 minutes, or until both sides are golden brown and the cheese is

melted.
Step 5.
Repeat with remaining tortillas, cooking in batches as needed. Serve.

Storage: Store any leftovers in an airtight container and refrigerate for up to 5 days.

Protein swap: If you don't want to use black beans, fill these quesadillas with cooked lentils, crumbled tempeh, or pinto beans. You could also try scrambled eggs to make these for brunch over the weekend.

PER SERVING: Calories: 513; Total fat: 21g; Carbohydrates: 53g; Fiber: 10g; Protein: 26g; Calcium: 523mg; Vitamin D: 0mcg; Vitamin B_{12} : 0µg; Iron: 5mg; Zinc: 3mg

Pan-Roasted Nachos
MAKES 4 SERVINGS • PREP TIME: 5 MINUTES • COOK TIME: 10 MINUTES

Ingredients

- 1 (12-ounce) bag corn tortilla chips
- 1 (15-ounce) can black beans, drained and rinsed
- 1 jalapeño pepper, sliced (optional)
- 1 tablespoon ground cumin
- 1 tablespoon chili powder
- 1 tablespoon fresh lime juice
- ¼ teaspoon kosher salt
- 1½ cups shredded pepper jack cheese
- 1 avocado, peeled, pitted, and diced

Directions:
Step 1.
Preheat the oven to 400°F. Line a rimmed baking sheet with parchment.

Step 2.
Spread the tortilla chips in a single layer on the baking sheet.

Step 3.
In a medium bowl, stir together the beans, jalapeño (if using), cumin, chili powder, lime juice, and salt until well combined, and top the tortilla chips evenly with the mixture.

Step 4.
Sprinkle the chips with the cheese and bake for 10 minutes, or until the cheese is melted.

Step 5.
Top the nachos with diced avocado and serve immediately.

Change it Up: For a milder flavor, omit the jalapeño and use shredded cheddar cheese instead of pepper jack. You can also try nachos with cotija cheese if you see it at your supermarket.

PER SERVING: Calories: 775; Total fat: 40g; Carbohydrates: 82g; Fiber: 15g; Protein: 24g; Calcium: 472mg; Vitamin D: 0mcg; Vitamin B_{12}: 0µg; Iron: 5mg; Zinc: 4mg

Baked Potato Skins

MAKES 4 SERVINGS • PREP TIME: 10 MINUTES • COOK TIME: 20 MINUTES

Ingredients

- 4 medium russet potatoes
- 1 tablespoon grapeseed oil, plus extra for greasing the skillet
- ¼ teaspoon kosher salt
- ½ cup shredded pepper jack or cheddar cheese
- ¼ cup chopped fresh chives
- Plain Greek yogurt, for dipping (optional)

Directions:

Step 1.

Preheat the oven to 450°F. Pierce the potatoes with a fork, transfer them to a baking sheet, and bake for 30 minutes, or until you can easily pierce them with a fork.

Step 2.

Make sure the baked potatoes are cooled, then slice them in half lengthwise, and use a spoon to scoop out about half the potato in each half. Reserve the scooped-out potato for another recipe.

Step 3.

Brush the potato skins with the oil and sprinkle with the salt.

Step 4.

Lightly oil a large skillet and preheat it over medium heat. Arrange the potatoes, cut-side down, in the skillet and cook for 15 minutes, or until the bottoms turn golden brown.

Step 5.

Flip the potatoes over, sprinkle with the cheese, and cook until the cheese is melted.

Step 6.

Top the potato skins with the chopped chives and serve with the yogurt for dipping, if desired.

Storage: Wrap leftover potatoes in plastic or beeswax wrap and refrigerate up to 5 days.

Protein swaps: To make these potato skins dairy-free, sprinkle with nutritional yeast instead of using pepper jack or cheddar cheese. Top with diced avocado for a plant-based fat alternative, or dip potato skins in guacamole instead of Greek yogurt.

PER SERVING: Calories: 214; Total fat: 8g; Carbohydrates: 30g; Fiber: 4g; Protein: 7g; Calcium: 127mg; Vitamin D: 0mcg; Vitamin B_{12} : 0μg; Iron: 1mg; Zinc: 1mg

Vegan Party Platter

MAKES 8 SERVINGS • PREP TIME: 10 MINUTES • COOK TIME: 5 MINUTES

Ingredients

- 1 cup whole almonds
- ¼ cup olive oil
- 2 tablespoons balsamic vinegar
- 1 teaspoon dried thyme
- Kosher salt
- Freshly ground black pepper
- 1 cup olives of choice
- 1 cup Tofu Feta or store-bought tofu
- 1½ cups Classic Hummus or store-bought hummus
- Crackers or fresh bread
- Fresh fruit, such as berries or grapes

Directions:

Step 1.

Preheat the oven to 350°F. Line a baking sheet with parchment.

Step 2.

Spread the almonds on the baking sheet and bake for 5 minutes or until aromatic. Transfer the almonds to a large bowl and set aside.

Step 3.

In a small bowl, whisk together the olive oil, vinegar, thyme, and salt and pepper to taste.

Step 4.

Add the olives to the bowl and mix to fully coat.

Step 5.

On a large platter, arrange the toasted almonds, marinated olives, tofu feta, hummus, crackers or fresh bread, and fresh fruit. Serve.

Storage: Store the crackers and bread in a bag or airtight container at room temperature. Cover the rest of the platter with plastic or beeswax wrap and refrigerate for up to 5 days. You can also transfer individual portions to smaller airtight containers.

Change it Up: If you like the concept of a party-friendly snack platter, but want to feature more Mexican flavors, assemble a plate with tortilla chips, salsa, guacamole, pickled vegetables, and queso sauce.

PER SERVING: Calories: 390; Total fat: 33g; Carbohydrates: 20g; Fiber: 7g; Protein: 14g; Calcium: 212mg; Vitamin D: 0mcg; Vitamin B$_{12}$: 0µg; Iron: 5mg; Zinc: 3mg

Chocolate-Covered Mangos

MAKES 8 SERVINGS • PREP TIME: 10 MINUTES, PLUS 10 MINUTES TO CHILL • COOK TIME: 2 MINUTES

Ingredients

- ¼ cup coconut oil
- 2 tablespoons unsweetened cocoa powder
- 2 tablespoons Vanilla Almond Milk (or milk of choice)
- 1 tablespoon maple syrup
- 2 cups dried mangos
- Flaky salt or chili powder (optional)

Directions:

Step 1.

In a small saucepan, stir together the coconut oil, cocoa powder, almond milk, and maple syrup over low heat. Cook for 2 minutes, stirring constantly, until a uniform sauce forms. Turn off the heat.

Step 2.

Dip a piece of dried mango into the chocolate sauce and transfer it to a baking dish or container with a lid. Repeat with remaining mango pieces, arranging them in a single layer. Sprinkle the dipped mango with flaky salt or chili powder (if using) and chill the fruit in the refrigerator for at least 10 minutes, or until the chocolate is set.

Mix it up: There are endless ways to enjoy chocolate-dipped fruit. Try dried pineapple rings or fresh strawberries. You can also sprinkle the fruit with finely chopped nuts, coconut flakes, or cacao nibs for extra flavor and texture. The toppings will stick to the fruit as the chocolate coating hardens.

Storage: Store the coated fruit in an airtight container in the refrigerator for up to 1 week. If you have leftover chocolate sauce, allow it to harden on a piece of parchment or a silicone baking mat. Then transfer it to a bag or container and store it in the refrigerator for up to 1 week.

PER SERVING: Calories: 145; Total fat: 7g; Carbohydrates: 22g; Fiber: 2g; Protein: 1g; Calcium: 19mg; Vitamin D: 0mcg; Vitamin B$_{12}$: 0µg; Iron: 0mg; Zinc: 0mg

Strawberry-Banana Ice Cream

MAKES 2 SERVINGS • PREP TIME: 5 MINUTES

Ingredients

- 2 cups frozen banana slices (from 4 small bananas)
- 1 cup frozen strawberries
- ¼ cup Vanilla Almond Milk (or milk of choice), or more as needed
- ⅛ teaspoon kosher salt

OPTIONAL FOR SERVING

- ¾ cup Vegan Chocolate Sauce
- Chopped nuts

Directions:

Step 1.

Place the bananas, strawberries, almond milk, and salt in a blender or food processor and blend for 1 minute, or until smooth and creamy, scraping down the sides with a spatula as needed. If the mixture isn't blending well, add a little more almond milk and process again. The blend should be similar to the consistency of soft-serve ice cream.

Step 2.

Serve immediately with the chocolate sauce and chopped nuts, if desired.

Mix it up: Frozen bananas provide the creamy, cool texture for this vegan treat, but you can swap in all sorts of ingredients to change the flavor. Try cocoa powder, peanut butter, pitted cherries, or even matcha. Add any toppings you usually like to have on ice cream sundaes.

PER SERVING: Calories: 184; Total fat: 1g; Carbohydrates: 46g; Fiber: 6g; Protein: 2g; Calcium: 82mg; Vitamin D: 0mcg; Vitamin B_{12}: 0µg; Iron: 1mg; Zinc: 1mg

Chickpea Cookie Dough

MAKES 2 SERVINGS • PREP TIME: 5 MINUTES

Ingredients

- 1 (15-ounce) can chickpeas, drained and rinsed
- ¼ cup creamy peanut butter
- ¼ cup maple syrup
- 1 teaspoon vanilla extract
- ¼ teaspoon kosher salt
- ¼ cup chocolate chips or chocolate chunks (optional)

Directions:

Step 1.

Place the chickpeas, peanut butter, maple syrup, vanilla, and salt in a food processor and process for 1 minute, or until smooth and creamy.

Step 2.

Transfer the mixture to a medium bowl and add the chocolate chips, if desired.

Storage: Store the dough in an airtight container in the refrigerator for up to 1 week.

Protein swaps: Instead of peanut butter, use sunflower seed butter or tahini to make this nut-free. Creamy Almond Butter is another tasty option if you don't have any peanut butter on hand.

PER SERVING: Calories: 503; Total fat: 20g; Carbohydrates: 68g; Fiber: 11g; Protein: 18g; Calcium: 117mg; Vitamin D: 0mcg; Vitamin B$_{12}$: 0μg; Iron: 4mg; Zinc: 3mg

Yogurt-Dipped Strawberries

MAKES 2 SERVINGS • PREP TIME: 15 MINUTES, PLUS 30 MINUTES TO CHILL

Ingredients

- 2 cups fresh strawberries, rinsed
- ½ cup vanilla Greek yogurt (whole milk)
- ¼ cup finely chopped nuts, such as pecans or walnuts

Directions:

Step 1.

Dry the strawberries with a clean towel or paper towel.

Step 2.

Dip three-fourths of a strawberry into the yogurt. Place the dipped berry on a clean plate and sprinkle with some of the nuts. Repeat with the remaining strawberries.

Step 3.

Chill in the refrigerator for at least 30 minutes.

Storage: Store leftovers in an airtight container and refrigerate for up to 1 week.

Make it easier: Use pre-chopped nuts or omit the nuts completely to make this recipe a little bit easier. You can also use flavored yogurt to add interest without any additional ingredients.

PER SERVING: Calories: 178; Total fat: 12g; Carbohydrates: 16g; Fiber: 4g; Protein: 4g; Calcium: 107mg; Vitamin D: 0mcg; Vitamin B$_{12}$: 0μg; Iron: 1mg; Zinc: 1mg

Chocolate-Avocado Pudding

MAKES 2 SERVINGS • PREP TIME: 5 MINUTES, PLUS 2 HOURS TO CHILL

Ingredients

- 2 avocados, peeled and pitted
- ¼ cup unsweetened cocoa powder
- ¼ cup maple syrup
- ½ teaspoon vanilla extract (optional)
- ⅛ teaspoon kosher salt

OPTIONAL FOR SERVING

- Whipped cream
- Chocolate chips or cacao nibs
- Fresh fruit

Directions:

Step 1.

Place the avocados, cocoa powder, maple syrup, vanilla, and salt in a blender or food processor and blend on high for 1 minute, or until smooth and creamy.

Step 2.

Transfer the pudding to 6-ounce ramekins or small bowls, cover, and chill in the refrigerator for at least 2 hours.

Step 3.

Serve with whipped cream, chocolate chips or cacao nibs, or fresh fruit, if desired.

Mix it up: Add any ingredients that pair well with chocolate to give this plant-based pudding a little more flavor appeal. Try blending in a little fresh mint, instant espresso powder, or fresh raspberries.

Storage: Cover the pudding with plastic wrap and refrigerate for up to 3 days.

PER SERVING: Calories: 491; Total fat: 32g; Carbohydrates: 56g; Fiber: 20g; Protein: 9g; Calcium: 83mg; Vitamin D: 0mcg; Vitamin B_{12} : 0µg; Iron: 2mg; Zinc: 2mg

Snickerdoodle Skillet Cookie

MAKES 8 SERVINGS • PREP TIME: 5 MINUTES • COOK TIME: 40 MINUTES

Ingredients

- Grapeseed oil or nonstick cooking spray

- ½ cup (packed) brown sugar
- ½ cup granulated sugar, plus additional for topping (optional)
- ¼ cup (½ stick) salted butter, melted
- 1 tablespoon ground cinnamon, plus extra for topping (optional)
- 1 large egg
- 1 teaspoon vanilla extract
- 1 cup all-purpose flour
- ¼ teaspoon baking soda

Directions:

Step 1.

Preheat the oven to 375°F. Grease a 10-inch oven-safe (cast iron or stainless steel) skillet.

Step 2.

In a large bowl, stir together the brown sugar, granulated sugar, butter, and cinnamon until there aren't any large lumps.

Step 3.

Add the egg and vanilla, stirring to combine.

Step 4.

Add the flour and baking soda and stir until a thick dough forms. Use your hands to mix at the end, if needed.

Step 5.

Press the dough firmly into the skillet, and sprinkle with additional granulated sugar and cinnamon, if desired.

Step 6.

Bake the cookie for 20 minutes, or until the edges are golden and the center is baked through. Allow the cookie to cool. Then serve it in the skillet or turn the skillet over to release to cookie and slice it into 8 wedges.

Storage: Wrap the cookie in plastic wrap or beeswax wrap and store in an airtight container at room temperature for up to 1 week.

Mix it up: Instead of cinnamon, try swapping in ½ cup chocolate chips. During the fall months, substitute pumpkin pie spice, which is made with cinnamon along with other warming spices such as ginger, nutmeg, and cloves.

PER SERVING: Calories: 221; Total fat: 7g; Carbohydrates: 39g; Fiber: 1g; Protein: 3g; Calcium: 29mg; Vitamin D: 0mcg; Vitamin B_{12}: 0µg; Iron: 1mg; Zinc: 0mg

Chocolate–Peanut Butter Cups

MAKES 12 SERVINGS • PREP TIME: 15 MINUTES, PLUS 1 HOUR TO CHILL

Ingredients

- ¼ cup sugar
- 1 teaspoon cornstarch
- 1 cup peanut butter
- 2½ cups chocolate chips, melted (dairy-free, if desired)
- Flaky salt (optional)

Directions:

Step 1.
Line a 12-cup muffin tin with paper liners and set it aside.

Step 2.
Place the sugar, cornstarch, and peanut butter in a food processor and process on high for 30 seconds or until the mixture is smooth and creamy.

Step 3.
Evenly divide half the melted chocolate among the muffin cups, spreading it evenly in the bottom of each one, about 1½ tablespoons in each cup.

Step 4.
Divide the peanut butter mixture among the cups, spooning it on top of the chocolate. Evenly divide the remaining melted chocolate among the cups to cover the peanut butter mixture.

Step 5.
Sprinkle the cups with flaky salt (if using) and chill them in the refrigerator for at least 1 hour, or until the chocolate is set.

Step 6.
Pull out the liners or run a knife around the edges to release each of the peanut butter cups.

Storage: Place the cups in an airtight container and store in the refrigerator for up to 1 month or freeze for up to 3 months.

Tip: Instead of peanut butter, use sunflower seed butter for a nut-free alternative. This recipe will also work with any type of nut butter, so try cashew or almond butter.

PER SERVING: Calories: 339; Total fat: 22g; Carbohydrates: 31g; Fiber: 4g; Protein: 7g; Calcium: 30mg; Vitamin D: 0mcg; Vitamin B_{12} : 0µg; Iron: 3mg; Zinc: 1mg

Chai Tea Mug Cake

MAKES 1 SERVING • PREP TIME: 5 MINUTES • COOK TIME: 2 MINUTES

Ingredients

- ⅓ cup Vanilla Almond Milk (or milk of choice)
- 1 tea bag chai tea
- ⅓ cup whole wheat pastry flour (or other flour of choice)

- 1 tablespoon sugar
- ¼ teaspoon baking powder
- ¼ teaspoon ground cinnamon, plus additional for topping
- Pinch of salt
- 1½ tablespoons grapeseed oil

Directions:

Step 1.
Heat the milk in a 14-ounce or larger mug in the microwave for 30 seconds, or until hot.

Step 2.
Steep the chai tea in the warmed milk for 5 minutes.

Step 3.
While the tea is steeping, in a small bowl, stir together the flour, sugar, baking powder, cinnamon, and salt until blended.

Step 4.
Squeeze the tea bag into the mug, discard the tea bag, and stir the oil into the mug. Gradually add the flour mixture to the mug, stirring until just mixed. Sprinkle the batter with additional cinnamon, if desired. Microwave the mug cake for 1 minute, or until the cake is cooked through. Serve.

Substitute: If you don't have chai tea, mimic the flavors by adding ⅛ teaspoon each of ground cardamom and ground ginger to the warmed milk. You can also make this chocolate flavored by omitting the chai tea and cinnamon and instead adding a spoonful of cocoa powder to the warmed milk.

PER SERVING: Calories: 364; Total fat: 22g; Carbohydrates: 39g; Fiber: 5g; Protein: 6g; Calcium: 226mg; Vitamin D: 1mcg; Vitamin B$_{12}$: 1μg; Iron: 2mg; Zinc: 2mg

Pumpkin Pie Parfait Jars

MAKES 2 SERVINGS • PREP TIME: 10 MINUTES

Ingredients

- 1 (15-ounce) can pumpkin puree
- ¼ cup Vanilla Almond Milk (or milk of choice)
- 2 tablespoons maple syrup, plus additional for serving
- 1 tablespoon pumpkin pie spice
- ⅛ teaspoon kosher salt
- 1 cup vanilla Greek yogurt (dairy or dairy-free)
- 1 cup granola, such as Apple Pie Granola

Directions:

Step 1.

In a medium bowl, stir together the pumpkin puree, almond milk, maple syrup, pumpkin pie spice, and salt until well blended.

Step 2.

Layer ¼ cup of the pumpkin mixture in the bottom of 2 pint glass jars. Add a spoonful of the vanilla yogurt to each jar and sprinkle ¼ cup of the granola on top. Repeat layering until all the ingredients are used.

Step 3.

Serve immediately or cover and refrigerate the parfait jars for up to 3 days.

Substitute: For a sweeter and less tart flavor, use whipped cream instead of yogurt. Blend canned coconut milk for 5 minutes, or until thickened, to make a dairy-free alternative to whipped cream.

PER SERVING: Calories: 381; Total fat: 6g; Carbohydrates: 75g; Fiber: 11g; Protein: 12g; Calcium: 318mg; Vitamin D: 0mcg; Vitamin B_{12} : 1µg; Iron: 5mg; Zinc: 3mg

Vegan No-Bake Blueberry Cheesecake

MAKES 8 SERVINGS • PREP TIME: 40 MINUTES, PLUS 8 HOURS TO CHILL • COOK TIME: 10 MINUTES

Ingredients

- 2 cups raw cashews (about 10 ounces)
- 2 cups frozen blueberries
- 2 tablespoons sugar
- 1 teaspoon grated lemon zest
- 2 cups chopped pitted dates
- 1⅕ cups walnut halves and pieces
- ½ cup unsweetened coconut flakes
- ½ cup Vanilla Almond Milk (or milk of choice)
- ¼ cup fresh lemon juice
- ¼ cup maple syrup
- ¼ teaspoon salt

Directions:

Step 1.

Place the cashews in a medium bowl and cover by about 2 inches with water. Set aside to soak for 30 minutes.

Step 2.

In a large saucepan, heat the blueberries, sugar, and lemon zest over medium heat until softened, stirring often, about 10 minutes. Remove the saucepan from the heat.

Step 3.

Place the dates, walnuts, and coconut flakes in a blender or food processor and pulse until the ingredients are finely chopped and the mixture sticks together when pressed between your fingers.

Step 4.

Firmly press the dough into the bottom of a freezer-safe, 10-inch pie dish, spreading it to evenly cover the bottom.

Step 5.

Drain the cashews, rinse, and transfer them to a blender or food processor along with the almond milk, lemon juice, maple syrup, and salt. Cover and blend for 1 minute, or until smooth and creamy. Spread the cashew mixture evenly over the crust.

Step 6.

Spread the cooked blueberries on top of the cashew mixture. Cover with plastic or beeswax wrap and freeze the pie overnight. Thaw the pie for 15 minutes or more before cutting it into 8 slices and serving.

Storage: Cover the leftovers with plastic wrap or beeswax wrap and freeze for up to 3 weeks.

Mix it up: Skip the blueberries and make the cheesecake plain. You can also top it with Vegan Chocolate Sauce or chopped nuts and maple syrup. Stir chocolate chips into the cashew filling for extra flavor and texture.

PER SERVING: Calories: 508; Total fat: 30g; Carbohydrates: 58g; Fiber: 7g; Protein: 11g; Calcium: 88mg; Vitamin D: 0mcg; Vitamin B_{12} : 0μg; Iron: 4mg; Zinc: 3mg

Creamy Oat Milk

MAKES 4 SERVINGS (ABOUT 4 CUPS TOTAL) • PREP TIME: 10 MINUTES

Ingredients

- 1 cup old-fashioned rolled oats, rinsed
- 4 cups water
- ⅛ teaspoon salt

Directions:

Step 1.

Place the oats, water, and salt in a blender and blend on high for 1 minute.

Step 2.

Strain the mixture through a cheesecloth or nut milk bag into a pitcher or quart jar. Squeeze at the end to extract all the liquid.

Storage: Cover the pitcher or seal the jar and refrigerate for up to 5 days. Shake well before using.

Mix it up: Add ½ teaspoon of vanilla extract or 2 cups of strawberries to flavor the milk. If you typically like sweetened plant-based milk, add a spoonful of sugar, maple syrup, or honey to the blender.

PER SERVING: Calories: 80; Total fat: 3g; Carbohydrates: 11g; Fiber: 1g; Protein: 2g; Calcium: 460mg; Vitamin D: 4mcg; Vitamin B$_{12}$: 0µg; Iron: 1mg; Zinc: 0mg

Vanilla Almond Milk

MAKES 4 SERVINGS (ABOUT 4 CUPS TOTAL) • PREP TIME: 10 MINUTES

Ingredients

- 1 cup slivered almonds
- 4 cups water
- ½ teaspoon vanilla extract
- 1 teaspoon maple syrup (optional)
- ⅛ teaspoon salt

Directions:

Step 1.
Place the almonds, water, vanilla, maple syrup (if using), and salt in a blender and blend on high for 1 minute.

Step 2.
Strain the mixture through a cheesecloth or nut milk bag into a pitcher or quart jar. If you're using a nut milk bag, squeeze the bag with your hands to extract as much liquid as possible.

Storage: Cover the pitcher or seal the jar and refrigerate for up to 5 days. Shake well before using.

Protein swaps: Use another type of nut, such as cashews, walnuts, or macadamia nuts, to make this milk.

PER SERVING: Calories: 60; Total fat: 3g; Carbohydrates: 8g; Fiber: 0g; Protein: 1g; Calcium: 451mg; Vitamin D: 3mcg; Vitamin B$_{12}$: 0µg; Iron: 1mg; Zinc: 1mg

Apple Cider Vinaigrette

MAKES 2 SERVINGS (ABOUT ¼ CUP TOTAL) • PREP TIME: 5 MINUTES

Ingredients

- 3 tablespoons olive oil
- 1 tablespoon apple cider vinegar
- 1 teaspoon maple syrup or honey
- 3 garlic cloves, minced (about 1 tablespoon)
- ½ teaspoon onion powder
- ¼ teaspoon kosher salt
- ¼ teaspoon freshly ground black pepper

Directions:

Step 1.

In a small bowl, whisk together the olive oil, vinegar, maple syrup, garlic, onion powder, salt, and pepper until well blended.

Step 2.

Pour into a cruet to serve.

Storage: Store the vinaigrette in an airtight container in the refrigerator for up to 2 weeks.

Make it easier: Cut down on the prep time and skip the knife and cutting board by using 1½ teaspoons of garlic powder in place of the fresh cloves. Every ½ teaspoon of garlic powder is roughly equivalent to 1 garlic clove.

PER SERVING: Calories: 198; Total fat: 20g; Carbohydrates: 4g; Fiber: 0g; Protein: 0g; Calcium: 14mg; Vitamin D: 0mcg; Vitamin B_{12}: 0µg; Iron: 0mg; Zinc: 0mg

Sesame Ginger Dressing

MAKES 2 SERVINGS (ABOUT ¼ CUP TOTAL) • PREP TIME: 5 MINUTES

Ingredients

- 3 tablespoons toasted sesame oil
- 1 tablespoon rice vinegar
- 1 teaspoon soy sauce
- 1 teaspoon maple syrup or honey
- 1 (2-inch) piece of fresh ginger, peeled and grated
- 3 garlic cloves, minced
- 1 scallion, both white and green parts, chopped (optional)
- 1 teaspoon sesame seeds (optional)

Directions:

Step 1.

In a small bowl, whisk together the sesame oil, vinegar, soy sauce, maple syrup, ginger, garlic, and the scallion and sesame seeds (if using) until blended.

Step 2.

Pour into a cruet to serve.

Storage: Store the dressing in an airtight container in the refrigerator for up to 2 weeks.

Make it easier: If you want to whip up this dressing without having to make an extra trip to the store, use dry ingredients instead of fresh. Swap in ground ginger, garlic powder, and onion powder to get similar flavors from pantry staples.

PER SERVING: Calories: 200; Total fat: 20g; Carbohydrates: 4g; Fiber: 0g; Protein: 1g; Calcium: 13mg; Vitamin D: 0mcg; Vitamin B_{12} : 0µg; Iron: 0mg; Zinc: 0mg

Lemon Tahini Dressing

MAKES 2 SERVINGS (ABOUT ¾ CUP TOTAL) • PREP TIME: 5 MINUTES

Ingredients

- 2 tablespoons tahini
- 1 teaspoon grated lemon zest (optional)
- 1 tablespoon fresh lemon juice
- 3 garlic cloves, minced
- 1 teaspoon maple syrup or honey
- ¼ teaspoon kosher salt
- ⅛ teaspoon freshly ground black pepper
- 2 tablespoons water, or more as needed

Directions:

Step 1.

In a small bowl, whisk together the tahini, lemon zest (if using), lemon juice, garlic, maple syrup, salt, and pepper until blended. Gradually add the water as needed until the dressing thins to your desired consistency.

Step 2.

Pour into a cruet to serve.

Storage: Store the dressing in an airtight container in the refrigerator for up to 10 days.

Protein swaps: Including nuts and seeds in salad dressings is a convenient way to get more protein. Any nut or seed butter can be substituted for the tahini in this recipe. Try it with sunflower seed, almond, cashew, or peanut butter.

PER SERVING: Calories: 106; Total fat: 8g; Carbohydrates: 7g; Fiber: 2g; Protein: 3g; Calcium: 76mg; Vitamin D: 0mcg; Vitamin B_{12} : 0µg; Iron: 1mg; Zinc: 1mg

Spicy Peanut Sauce

MAKES 4 SERVINGS (ABOUT 1½ CUPS TOTAL) • PREP TIME: 10 MINUTES

Ingredients

- ¼ cup creamy peanut butter
- 2 tablespoons rice vinegar
- 1 tablespoon soy sauce
- 1 tablespoon maple syrup
- ½ teaspoon garlic powder
- ½ teaspoon ground ginger
- ¼ teaspoon cayenne
- 2 tablespoons water, or more as needed

Directions:

Step 1.

In a medium bowl, whisk together the peanut butter, vinegar, soy sauce, maple syrup, garlic powder, ginger, and cayenne until blended.

Step 2.

Gradually whisk in the water as needed until the desired consistency is reached.

Step 3.

Pour into a bowl, ready to serve.

Storage: Store the sauce in an airtight container in the refrigerator for up to 1 week.

Tip: If you don't have peanut butter, substitute almond butter, cashew butter, or tahini. Instead of maple syrup, use sugar, honey, or agave nectar. If you prefer, you can also omit the sweetener completely.

PER SERVING: Calories: 116; Total fat: 8g; Carbohydrates: 7g; Fiber: 1g; Protein: 4g; Calcium: 15mg; Vitamin D: 0mcg; Vitamin B_{12} : 0µg; Iron: 0mg; Zinc: 1mg

Rosemary and Thyme Red Sauce

MAKES 4 SERVINGS (ABOUT 3 CUPS TOTAL) • PREP TIME: 5 MINUTES • COOK TIME: 15 MINUTES

Ingredients

- 2 tablespoons grapeseed oil
- ½ cup diced onion (1 small)
- 6 garlic cloves, minced (or 3 teaspoons garlic powder)

- 1 tablespoon crushed fresh rosemary
- 1 tablespoon dried thyme
- ½ teaspoon kosher salt
- ¼ teaspoon freshly ground black pepper
- 1 (28-ounce) can crushed tomatoes, with juice
- 1 tablespoon maple syrup

Directions:

Step 1.

Heat the oil in a large saucepan over medium heat.

Step 2.

Once the oil is shiny, add the onion and cook for 4 minutes, or until translucent.

Step 3.

Add the garlic, rosemary, thyme, salt, and pepper and cook for 1 minute.

Step 4.

Add the tomatoes and maple syrup and bring the sauce to a boil. Reduce the heat to low and simmer the sauce for 10 minutes, stirring occasionally.

Step 5.

Cool the sauce for 5 minutes, then transfer to a quart jar with a lid.

Storage: Refrigerate the sauce for up to 4 days or place it in a freezer-save container and freeze for up to 6 months.

Mix it up: Add umami flavor to this Italian-inspired tomato sauce with a handful of grated Parmesan cheese. Instead of rosemary and thyme, try seasoning the sauce with basil, oregano, marjoram, or sage.

PER SERVING: Calories: 120; Total fat: 7g; Carbohydrates: 14g; Fiber: 5g; Protein: 2g; Calcium: 90mg; Vitamin D: 0mcg; Vitamin B_{12} : 0µg; Iron: 1mg; Zinc: 0mg

Chimichurri Sauce

MAKES 2 SERVINGS (ABOUT ½ CUP TOTAL) • PREP TIME: 15 MINUTES

Ingredients

- ¼ cup olive oil
- 2 tablespoons finely chopped fresh parsley
- 2 tablespoons finely chopped fresh cilantro
- 2 tablespoons red wine vinegar
- 2 garlic cloves, minced
- ¼ teaspoon red pepper flakes
- ¼ teaspoon kosher salt

- ¼ teaspoon freshly ground black pepper

Directions:

Step 1.

In a medium bowl, whisk together the olive oil, parsley, cilantro, vinegar, garlic, red pepper flakes, salt, and pepper until well mixed.

Step 2.

Pour into a bowl, ready to serve.

Storage: Store the sauce in an airtight container in the refrigerator for up to 3 weeks.

Mix it up: For extra texture, along with some additional gut-boosting fiber, essential fatty acids, and satisfying protein, try stirring in a spoonful of hemp hearts or finely chopped walnuts.

PER SERVING: Calories: 248; Total fat: 27g; Carbohydrates: 1g; Fiber: 0g; Protein: 0g; Calcium: 13mg; Vitamin D: 0mcg; Vitamin B_{12} : 0μg; Iron: 1mg; Zinc: 0mg

Carrot-Top Pesto

MAKES 4 SERVINGS (ABOUT 1¼ CUPS TOTAL) • PREP TIME: 5 MINUTES

Ingredients

- ½ cup carrot greens
- ½ cup fresh basil
- ¼ cup walnut halves and pieces
- 4 garlic cloves, chopped
- ¼ cup shredded Parmesan cheese
- 1 tablespoon fresh lemon juice
- 1 teaspoon maple syrup
- ¼ teaspoon kosher salt
- ¼ teaspoon freshly ground black pepper
- 6 tablespoons olive oil

Directions:

Step 1.

Place the carrot greens, basil, walnuts, garlic, Parmesan, lemon juice, maple syrup, salt, and pepper in a food processor and process until the ingredients are finely chopped.

Step 2.

Pour in the olive oil and pulse until the desired consistency is reached.

Step 3.

Pour into a jar with a lid until ready to serve.

Storage: Store the pesto in an airtight container in the refrigerator for up to 4 days or freeze for up to 4 months.

Substitute: Use nutritional yeast instead of Parmesan cheese to make this pesto vegan and dairy-free. Use sunflower seeds instead of walnuts to make it nut-free. If you don't have carrot tops, substitute with additional basil or fresh parsley.

PER SERVING: Calories: 264; Total fat: 27g; Carbohydrates: 4g; Fiber: 1g; Protein: 3g; Calcium: 76mg; Vitamin D: 0mcg; Vitamin B$_{12}$: 0µg; Iron: 1mg; Zinc: 1mg

Spicy Blender Salsa

MAKES 8 SERVINGS (ABOUT 3 CUPS TOTAL) • PREP TIME: 10 MINUTES

Ingredients

- 3 ripe medium tomatoes (1 pound)
- ½ cup chopped onion
- 4 garlic cloves, chopped
- ⅓ cup chopped fresh cilantro
- 1 jalapeño pepper, chopped (optional)
- ¼ lime
- ¼ teaspoon kosher salt

Directions:

Step 1.
Place the tomatoes, onion, garlic, cilantro, jalapeño, lime, and salt in a blender and blend on high for 15 seconds or until the desired consistency is reached.

Step 2.
Pour into a jar with a lid.

Storage: Store in an airtight container in the refrigerator for up to 2 weeks.

Substitute: Substitute a 28-ounce can of tomatoes for the fresh tomatoes to make this salsa during the winter months. You can also make salsa verde (green salsa) by substituting fresh tomatillos for the tomatoes.

PER SERVING: Calories: 15; Total fat: 0g; Carbohydrates: 3g; Fiber: 1g; Protein: 1g; Calcium: 10mg; Vitamin D: 0mcg; Vitamin B$_{12}$: 0µg; Iron: 0mg; Zinc: 0mg

Chunky Guacamole

MAKES 8 SERVINGS (ABOUT 3 CUPS TOTAL) • PREP TIME: 10 MINUTES

Ingredients

- 4 medium avocados, peeled and pitted
- 1 ripe medium tomato, diced
- ⅓ cup chopped fresh cilantro
- ¼ cup minced red onion
- 1 jalapeño pepper, minced
- 1 teaspoon grated lime zest
- 1 tablespoon fresh lime juice
- ¼ teaspoon kosher salt

Directions:

Step 1.

In a medium bowl, mash the avocados with a potato masher or a fork until they are the desired consistency.

Step 2.

Add the tomato, cilantro, red onion, jalapeño, lime zest, lime juice, and salt and stir to combine. Best served immediately.

Mix it up: For a crunchy twist, try mixing in chopped jicama. Jicama is a white tuber that has a crisp texture and sweet, nutty flavor. You can also use jicama strips for dipping in guacamole.

PER SERVING: Calories: 189; Total fat: 15g; Carbohydrates: 13g; Fiber: 9g; Protein: 4g; Calcium: 19mg; Vitamin D: 0mcg; Vitamin B_{12} : 0μg; Iron: 0mg; Zinc: 1mg

Vegan Queso Dip

MAKES 2 SERVINGS (ABOUT 1 CUP TOTAL) • PREP TIME: 35 MINUTES • COOK TIME: 5 MINUTES

Ingredients

- ¼ cup raw sunflower seeds
- ½ cup plain unsweetened oat milk (or milk of choice)
- 1 tablespoon nutritional yeast
- 2 chipotle chiles in adobo sauce
- ½ teaspoon onion powder
- ½ teaspoon garlic powder
- ¼ teaspoon kosher salt
- ⅛ teaspoon freshly ground black pepper
- 2 tablespoons water, or more as needed

Directions:

Step 1.

Place the sunflower seeds in a small bowl and cover with water by about 1 inch. Set aside to soak for 30 minutes.

Step 2.

Drain the sunflower seeds and transfer them to a blender or food processor. Add the milk, nutritional yeast, chipotle chiles, onion powder, garlic powder, salt, and pepper. Blend for 1 minute, or until the sauce is smooth and creamy. If the mixture is too thick, add the water and blend again.

Step 3.

Transfer the sauce to a small saucepan and place it over medium heat. Cook the sauce for 5 minutes, or until warmed through.

Step 4.

Pour into a bowl, ready to serve.

Mix it up: If you don't have canned chipotle peppers in adobo sauce, substitute with 1 teaspoon of chili powder and cayenne to taste. You can also add black beans, sliced jalapeño peppers, or fresh cilantro.

PER SERVING: Calories: 168; Total fat: 10g; Carbohydrates: 14g; Fiber: 3g; Protein: 8g; Calcium: 103mg; Vitamin D: 1mcg; Vitamin B_{12} : 1µg; Iron: 2mg; Zinc: 2mg

Classic Hummus

MAKES 4 SERVINGS (ABOUT 1½ CUPS TOTAL) • PREP TIME: 5 MINUTES

Ingredients

- 1¼ cups cooked or canned chickpeas
- ¼ cup tahini
- 3 garlic cloves, chopped
- 1 tablespoon grated lemon zest
- 2 tablespoons fresh lemon juice
- 2 tablespoons olive oil, or more as needed
- ¼ teaspoon kosher salt
- ⅛ teaspoon freshly ground black pepper
- Smoked paprika (optional)

Directions:

Step 1.

Place the chickpeas, tahini, garlic, lemon zest, lemon juice, olive oil, salt, and pepper in a food processor and process for 1 minute or until smooth and creamy. If the mixture is too thick or isn't mixing, add another tablespoon of olive oil and process again.

Step 2.

Transfer the hummus to a bowl and sprinkle it with smoked paprika, if desired, and serve.

Protein swaps: Traditional hummus is made with chickpeas, but you can use any type of pulse to make a protein-packed dip or sandwich spread like this one. Try substituting lentils, cannellini beans, or navy beans.

Storage: Store the hummus in an airtight container in the refrigerator for up to 1 week.

PER SERVING: Calories: 239; Total fat: 16g; Carbohydrates: 19g; Fiber: 4g; Protein: 7g; Calcium: 94mg; Vitamin D: 0mcg; Vitamin B_{12} : 0µg; Iron: 3mg; Zinc: 2mg

White Bean Sandwich Spread

MAKES 2 SERVINGS (ABOUT 1 CUP TOTAL) • PREP TIME: 5 MINUTES

Ingredients

- 1 (15-ounce) can cannellini beans, drained and rinsed
- 1 teaspoon grated lemon zest
- 1 tablespoon fresh lemon juice
- 1 tablespoon olive oil, or more as needed
- 1 tablespoon nutritional yeast (optional)
- 1 teaspoon onion powder
- 2 garlic cloves, minced
- ¼ teaspoon kosher salt
- ¼ teaspoon freshly ground black pepper

Directions:

Step 1.

Place the beans, lemon zest, lemon juice, olive oil, nutritional yeast (if using), onion powder, garlic, salt, and pepper in the food processor and process for 1 minute, or until smooth and creamy.

Step 2.

If the mixture is too thick, add a tablespoon of olive oil or water and process again.

Step 3.

Pour into a jar with a lid.

Mix it up: Nutritional yeast adds a cheesy flavor to this white bean spread, but you can also flavor it with basil, oregano, Jamaican jerk, Cajun seasoning, or curry powder. If you don't have cannellini beans, try substituting navy beans or lentils.

Storage: Store the spread in an airtight container in the refrigerator for up to 1 week.

PER SERVING: Calories: 239; Total fat: 7g; Carbohydrates: 33g; Fiber: 9g; Protein: 12g;

Calcium: 58mg; Vitamin D: 0mcg; Vitamin B$_{12}$: 0µg; Iron: 3mg; Zinc: 1mg

Almond Ricotta

MAKES 4 SERVINGS (ABOUT 1 CUP TOTAL) • PREP TIME: 5 MINUTES

Ingredients

- 2 cups slivered almonds
- 1 tablespoon nutritional yeast
- 2 tablespoons fresh lemon juice
- ¼ teaspoon onion powder
- ¼ teaspoon garlic powder
- ½ teaspoon kosher salt

Directions:

1. Place the almonds, nutritional yeast, lemon juice, onion powder, garlic powder, and salt in a blender and blend on high for 1 minute, pausing to scrape down the sides with a spatula as needed, or until smooth and creamy.

Storage: Store the ricotta in an airtight container in the refrigerator for up to 1 week.

Mix it up: Try stirring in fresh or dried herbs, such as basil, oregano, rosemary, thyme, marjoram, or sage. You can also mix in dried Italian seasoning to give this plant-based cheese some extra herbaceous flavor.

PER SERVING: Calories: 324; Total fat: 27g; Carbohydrates: 13g; Fiber: 7g; Protein: 13g; Calcium: 149mg; Vitamin D: 0mcg; Vitamin B$_{12}$: 0µg; Iron: 2mg; Zinc: 2mg

Tofu Feta

MAKES 2 SERVINGS (ABOUT 1 CUP TOTAL) • PREP TIME: 5 MINUTES, PLUS 30 MINUTES TO MARINATE

Ingredients

- 1 (14-ounce) block firm tofu
- 3 tablespoons olive oil
- 1 teaspoon grated lemon zest
- 1 tablespoon fresh lemon juice
- 1 tablespoon nutritional yeast
- 1 teaspoon garlic powder
- 1 teaspoon dried oregano
- ¼ teaspoon kosher salt

- ⅛ teaspoon freshly ground black pepper

Directions:

Step 1.

Use your hands to crumble the tofu into a large bowl.

Step 2.

Add the olive oil, lemon zest, lemon juice, nutritional yeast, garlic powder, dried oregano, salt, and pepper to the bowl, mixing to combine.

Step 3.

Marinate the tofu for at least 30 minutes at room temperature or in the refrigerator overnight.

Storage: Store the tofu feta in an airtight container in the refrigerator for up to 3 days.

Mix it up: This vegan feta cheese is marinated with dried oregano for herbaceous Mediterranean flavor. Omit the oregano if you'd like this tofu feta to be unflavored. You can also add additional herbs and spices, such as basil, thyme, or red pepper flakes.

PER SERVING: Calories: 385; Total fat: 32g; Carbohydrates: 8g; Fiber: 2g; Protein: 22g; Calcium: 365mg; Vitamin D: 0mcg; Vitamin B$_{12}$: 0μg; Iron: 4mg; Zinc: 3mg

Blueberry Chia Jam

MAKES 8 SERVINGS (ABOUT 2 CUPS TOTAL) • PREP TIME: 5 MINUTES • COOK TIME: 15 MINUTES

Ingredients

- 2 cups fresh or frozen blueberries
- ½ cup maple syrup
- 2 tablespoons chia seeds
- 1 tablespoon fresh lemon juice
- ⅛ teaspoon salt

Directions:

Step 1.

In a large saucepan, stir together the blueberries, maple syrup, chia seeds, lemon juice, and salt over medium heat.

Step 2.

Cook the mixture for 15 minutes or until the blueberries are softened and the jam is thickened. The jam will continue to thicken as it cools.

Storage: Store the cooled jam in an airtight container in the refrigerator for up to 1 month.

Mix it up: Instead of blueberries, make homemade chia jam with blackberries, strawberries, or raspberries during the spring and summer. In fall and winter months, try making this jam with apples or pears.

PER SERVING: Calories: 90; Total fat: 1g; Carbohydrates: 20g; Fiber: 2g; Protein: 1g; Calcium: 45mg; Vitamin D: 0mcg; Vitamin B_{12}: 0µg; Iron: 0mg; Zinc: 0mg

Creamy Almond Butter

MAKES 8 SERVINGS (ABOUT 1 CUP TOTAL) • PREP TIME: 15 MINUTES • COOK TIME: 5 MINUTES

Ingredients

- 1 cup blanched almonds
- 1 tablespoon coconut oil
- ¼ teaspoon kosher salt

Directions:

Step 1.
Preheat the oven or toaster oven to 350°F. Line a baking sheet with parchment.

Step 2.
Spread the almonds on the baking sheet and bake for 5 minutes, or until golden and aromatic.

Step 3.
Transfer the almonds to a food processor and process for 10 minutes, or until smooth, creamy, and thickened. Pause to scrape down the sides with a spatula as needed. Once the almond butter is thick, add the coconut oil and salt and process for 15 seconds to mix.

Mix it up: Use this creamy nut butter recipe as the base for all types of sweet flavors. Some of my favorite ingredients to mix into this creamy almond butter are cocoa powder, vanilla, and cinnamon. Add any of these with the coconut oil and salt at the end of processing.

Storage: Store the almond butter in an airtight container in the refrigerator for up to 1 month.

PER SERVING: Calories: 118; Total fat: 11g; Carbohydrates: 4g; Fiber: 2g; Protein: 4g; Calcium: 48mg; Vitamin D: 0mcg; Vitamin B_{12}: 0µg; Iron: 1mg; Zinc: 1mg

Whole-Grain Croutons

MAKES 4 SERVINGS (ABOUT 1 CUP TOTAL) • PREP TIME: 5 MINUTES • COOK TIME: 15 MINUTES

Ingredients

- 2 cups torn whole-grain bread

- 2 tablespoons grapeseed oil, or other oil of choice
- 1 tablespoon nutritional yeast (optional)
- 1 teaspoon dried thyme
- ½ teaspoon onion powder
- ½ teaspoon garlic powder
- ½ teaspoon kosher salt
- ¼ teaspoon freshly ground black pepper

Directions:

Step 1.

Preheat the oven or toaster oven to 375°F. Line a baking sheet with parchment.

Step 2.

In a large bowl, toss together the bread, oil, nutritional yeast (if using), thyme, onion powder, garlic powder, salt, and pepper, and spread the mixture out in a single layer on the baking sheet.

Step 3.

Bake the croutons for 15 minutes or until golden and crispy. Cool them on a rack before serving.

Storage: Store the croutons in an airtight container at room temperature for up to 1 week.

Make it easier: To make plain whole-grain croutons, skip the nutritional yeast, thyme, onion powder, and garlic powder. Toss the torn bread pieces with oil, salt, and pepper, and bake as described.

PER SERVING: Calories: 114; Total fat: 8g; Carbohydrates: 9g; Fiber: 2g; Protein: 3g; Calcium: 22mg; Vitamin D: 0mcg; Vitamin B_{12} : 0μg; Iron: 1mg; Zinc: 0mg

Vegan Chocolate Sauce

MAKES 4 SERVINGS (ABOUT ¾ CUP TOTAL) • PREP TIME: 5 MINUTES • COOK TIME: 5 MINUTES

Ingredients

- ½ cup Vanilla Almond Milk (or milk of choice)
- ½ cup unsweetened cocoa powder
- ¼ cup maple syrup
- ⅛ teaspoon salt

Directions:

Step 1.

In a medium saucepan, whisk together the almond milk, cocoa powder, maple syrup, and salt over medium-low heat.

Step 2.

Simmer the sauce for 5 minutes, or until warmed through, stirring constantly. Remove the sauce from the heat.

Storage: Store the sauce in an airtight container in the refrigerator for up to 1 week. Shake well before using.

Substitute: Instead of almond milk, substitute oat milk, hemp milk, or flax milk to make this chocolate sauce nut-free. If you include dairy products in your lifestyle, you can also make this recipe with cow's milk.

PER SERVING: Calories: 88; Total fat: 2g; Carbohydrates: 21g; Fiber: 3g; Protein: 3g; Calcium: 68mg; Vitamin D: 0mcg; Vitamin B_{12} : 0µg; Iron: 2mg; Zinc: 1mg
and hiking with her husband in the mountains.

Cinnamon Oat Milk Latte

MAKES 1 SERVING • PREP TIME: 3 MINUTES • COOK TIME: 1 MINUTE 30 SECONDS

Ingredients

- 1 cup unsweetened Creamy Oat Milk
- 1 teaspoon maple syrup (optional for sweetness; omit if oat milk is already sweetened)
- ½ teaspoon ground cinnamon, plus additional for topping
- ½ cup hot brewed espresso coffee or strong brewed dark coffee

Directions:

Step 1.

Stir together the oat milk, maple syrup, and cinnamon in a large, microwave-safe mug or bowl. (It's okay if the cinnamon doesn't fully incorporate into the oat milk before it's heated.)

Step 2.

Cover with a paper towel and microwave on high for 1 minute 30 seconds or until hot.

Step 3.

Whisk vigorously with a small whisk or fork to froth the milk and fully incorporate the cinnamon into the oat milk.

Step 4.

Add the brewed espresso coffee.

Step 5.

Sprinkle with additional cinnamon, if desired.

Substitute: You can use any type of milk for this recipe. If you're looking for a latte with plant-based protein, try soy milk. It's one of the only dairy-free milk alternatives that has as much protein as cow's milk.

PER SERVING (1 CUP): Calories: 80; Total fat: 3g; Carbohydrates: 11g; Fiber: 1g; Protein: 2g; Calcium: 460mg; Vitamin D: 4mcg; Vitamin B_{12}: 0µg; Iron: 1mg; Zinc: 0mg

Rejuvenating Citrus Smoothie

MAKES 2 SERVINGS • PREP TIME: 10 MINUTES

Ingredients

- 3 cups frozen mango chunks
- 1 cup unsweetened soy milk (or milk of choice)
- 4 teaspoons grated orange zest
- Juice of 2 large oranges
- 4 tablespoons ground flaxseed
- ½ teaspoon ground ginger (optional)

Directions:

Step 1.

Place the mango, soy milk, orange zest, orange juice, ground flaxseed, and ginger (if using) in a blender.

Step 2.

Cover and blend on high for 30 seconds, or until smooth and creamy.

Step 3.

If the consistency is too thick, add more soy milk or orange juice, cover, and blend again. If the consistency is too thin, add more ground flaxseed or frozen mango chunks, cover, and blend again.

Tip: If you want to cut out some of the preparation steps to make this recipe quicker and easier, omit the grated orange zest and use bottled orange juice instead of fresh oranges.

PER SERVING: Calories: 348; Total fat: 11g; Carbohydrates: 58g; Fiber: 10g; Protein: 11g; Calcium: 242mg; Vitamin D: 2mcg; Vitamin B_{12}: 1µg; Iron: 2mg; Zinc: 2mg

No-Bake Green Tea Energy Bars

MAKES 8 BARS • PREP TIME: 15 MINUTES, PLUS 1 HOUR TO FREEZE

Ingredients

- 1¼ cups chopped pitted dates

- ¾ cup walnut halves and pieces
- ½ cup whole almonds
- 2 tablespoons ground flaxseed
- 1 tablespoon matcha
- 1 tablespoon vanilla extract
- ¼ teaspoon kosher salt

Directions:

Step 1.
Combine the dates, walnuts, almonds, ground flaxseed, matcha, vanilla, and salt in a food processor.

Step 2.
Pulse 10 times, scraping down the sides with a spatula as needed, or until the mixture sticks together when pressed between your fingers.

Step 3.
Transfer the dough to an 8-inch square baking dish (or similarly sized pan) lined with parchment paper or aluminum foil. (This makes the bars easier to remove later on.)

Step 4.
Cover with plastic wrap and freeze overnight or for at least 1 hour.

Step 5.
Remove the baking dish from the freezer and carefully lift out the parchment paper or aluminum foil to remove the nut mixture.

Step 6.
Slide the nut mixture onto a cutting board and slice into 8 rectangular pieces. Serve.

Storage: Cover or wrap each bar separately and refrigerate for up to 2 weeks or freeze for up to 3 months.

Mix it up: You can use this basic recipe to make all sorts of energy bar flavors. Instead of matcha, try mixing in a tablespoon of cinnamon, pumpkin pie spice, or cocoa powder.

PER SERVING (1 BAR): Calories: 202; Total fat: 12g; Carbohydrates: 21g; Fiber: 4g; Protein: 4g; Calcium: 48mg; Vitamin D: 0mcg; Vitamin B_{12}: 0μg; Iron: 1mg; Zinc: 1mg

Spicy Chickpea-Avocado Toast

MAKES 2 SERVINGS • PREP TIME: 10 MINUTES • COOK TIME: 2 MINUTES

Ingredients

- 2 slices whole-grain bread
- 1 avocado, peeled and pitted
- 1 (15-ounce) can chickpeas, drained and rinsed

- 2 tablespoons fresh lemon juice
- ¼ teaspoon cayenne
- ½ teaspoon nutritional yeast (optional)
- Kosher salt

Directions:

Step 1.

Toast the bread in a toaster or toaster oven for 1 to 2 minutes. If you don't have a toaster, brown the bread under the broiler in the oven or in a greased skillet on a hot plate burner.

Step 2.

In a small bowl, mash the avocado and chickpeas together.

Step 3.

Add the lemon juice, cayenne, nutritional yeast (if using), and salt.

Step 4.

Spread the chickpea mixture on each piece of the toasted bread. Serve immediately.

Tip: If you don't have chickpeas, try swapping in canned cannellini beans because they have a smooth, creamy texture that makes them ideal for mashing and pureeing.

PER SERVING: Calories: 457; Total fat: 20g; Carbohydrates: 58g; Fiber: 20g; Protein: 18g; Calcium: 104mg; Vitamin D: 0mcg; Vitamin B$_{12}$: 0μg; Iron: 4mg; Zinc: 3mg

Apple Pie Granola

MAKES 12 SERVINGS • PREP TIME: 10 MINUTES • COOK TIME: 50 MINUTES

Ingredients

- 3 cups old-fashioned rolled oats
- 1 cup walnut or pecan halves (or a mix of both)
- 2 tablespoons sugar
- 1 tablespoon ground cinnamon
- 1 teaspoon ground allspice
- 1 teaspoon ground ginger
- ½ teaspoon kosher salt
- 6 dates, pitted and chopped
- ½ cup unsweetened applesauce
- ¼ cup olive oil
- ¼ cup maple syrup

Directions:

Step 1.

Preheat the oven to 325°F.

Step 2.

In a large bowl, stir together the oats, walnuts, sugar, cinnamon, allspice, ginger, and salt until well mixed.

Step 3.

Add the dates and stir to mix.

Step 4.

Add the applesauce, olive oil, and maple syrup, stirring until everything is evenly coated.

Step 5.

Transfer the mixture to a baking sheet and bake for 50 minutes, stirring every 10 to 15 minutes, or until the edges are golden brown.

Step 6.

Cool the granola for at least 10 minutes before serving. Granola gets crispier as it cools.

Storage: Store the granola in an airtight container in a cool, dry area for up to 6 months.

Tip: If you have a nut allergy or want to make this recipe more affordable, try substituting seeds for the walnuts and pecans. Pumpkin and sunflower seeds are budget-friendly and work great in homemade granola.

PER SERVING: Calories: 297; Total fat: 14g; Carbohydrates: 38g; Fiber: 6g; Protein: 8g; Calcium: 47mg; Vitamin D: 0mcg; Vitamin B_{12} : 0μg; Iron: 2mg; Zinc: 2mg

Peanut Butter and Banana Overnight Oats

MAKES 2 SERVINGS • PREP TIME: 5 MINUTES, PLUS 8 HOURS TO CHILL

Ingredients

- 1 cup old-fashioned rolled oats
- 1 cup soy milk (or milk of choice)
- 1 medium banana, sliced
- 2 tablespoons peanut butter
- 1 teaspoon ground cinnamon
- ¼ teaspoon kosher salt (omit if peanut butter contains salt)

OPTIONAL TOPPINGS

- Maple syrup
- Chopped peanuts
- Cacao nibs or chocolate chips

Directions:

Step 1.

Divide the oats, soy milk, banana, peanut butter, cinnamon, and salt (if using) between 2 jars and stir to mix.

Step 2.

Top with the maple syrup, peanuts, and cacao nibs or chocolate chips, if desired.

Step 3.

Seal the jars and refrigerate overnight.

Tip: Substitute tahini (sesame seed paste) or sunflower seed butter and omit the chopped peanuts if you have a peanut allergy. Almond or cashew butter also works well if you're able to tolerate nuts in your diet.

PER SERVING: Calories: 506; Total fat: 15g; Carbohydrates: 76g; Fiber: 11g; Protein: 22g; Calcium: 219mg; Vitamin D: 2mcg; Vitamin B_{12}: 1μg; Iron: 4mg; Zinc: 4mg

Tropical Chia Pudding Parfait

MAKES 2 SERVINGS • PREP TIME: 10 MINUTES, PLUS 8 HOURS TO CHILL

Ingredients

- 1½ cups unsweetened soy milk (or milk of choice)
- ⅓ cup chia seeds
- 2 teaspoons vanilla extract
- 2 teaspoons maple syrup (omit if milk is sweetened)
- ⅛ teaspoon kosher salt
- 1 cup frozen mango chunks, thawed
- 1 cup frozen pineapple chunks, thawed
- ½ cup unsweetened coconut flakes

Directions:

Step 1.

In a medium bowl, whisk the soy milk, chia seeds, vanilla, maple syrup, and salt together until well mixed.

Step 2.

Cover the bowl and refrigerate overnight.

Step 3.

Divide one-half of the chia mixture between 2 jars.

Step 4.

Divide one-half of the mango, pineapple, and coconut flakes between the jars.

Step 5.

Divide the remaining chia mixture between the jars.

Step 6.

Add the remaining mango, pineapple, and coconut flakes to each jar. Serve.

Storage: Seal the jars and refrigerate for up to 1 week.

Tip: Mix up the fruit to create different flavor profiles for the chia pudding parfaits. Instead of the tropical fruits, try substituting berries (blueberries, raspberries, blackberries, or sliced strawberries) or sliced banana.

PER SERVING: Calories: 444; Total fat: 21g; Carbohydrates: 55g; Fiber: 17g; Protein: 12g; Calcium: 470mg; Vitamin D: 3mcg; Vitamin B_{12}: 2μg; Iron: 4mg; Zinc: 3mg

Printed in Great Britain
by Amazon